W9-BON-578

FINAL CELEBRATIONS

A Guide For Personal and Family Funeral Planning

FINAL CELEBRATIONS
A Guide For Personal and Family Funeral Planning

By

Kathleen Sublette and Martin Flagg

Pathfinder Publishing of California
Ventura, CA

FINAL CELEBRATIONS:

A Guide for Personal and Family Funeral Planning

By

Kathleen Sublette and Martin Flagg

Edited by Eugene D. Wheeler

Published By:
Pathfinder Publishing of California
3600 Harbor Blvd #82
Oxnard, CA 93035
(805) 984-7756

All rights reserved. No part of this book may be reproduced or transmitted in any form or by any means, electronic or mechanical, including photocopying, recording or by any information storage and retrieval system without written permission from the authors, except for the inclusion of brief quotations in a review.

Copyright © 1992 by Kathleen Sublette & Martin Flagg
2nd Printing
Library of Congress Cataloging-in-Publication Data
Sublette, Kathleen, 1942-
    Final celebrations : a guide for personal and family funeral planning
/ by Kathleen Sublette and Martin Flagg.
        p. cm.
    Includes bibliographical references and index.
    ISBN 0-934793-43-3 : $9.95
        1. Funeral rites and ceremonies – United States – Handbooks,
manual, etc. I. Flagg, Martin, 1962-   . II. Title.
    GT3203.S8   1992
    393' .9 – dc20   91-44568
                                        CIP

ISBN 0-934793-43-3

DEDICATION

TO: those who dare to look ahead and all those who provide physical and emotional support to the terminally ill and their survivors.

Personal Dedications

By Kathleen Sublette - To my mother, who taught me how to celebrate life.

By Martin Flagg - To James S. Flagg, my father, for sharing his leadership and knowledge with me.

Acknowledgments

Our thanks go to many for reviewing and commenting on the manuscript including: Joyce Dace-Lombard, Lou Hartney, Herb Mucktarian, Ann Shields, Kathy Stinson, Julie Tilsner, Douglas Werner, Eugenie G. Wheeler, Nancy and Pete Wygle. Their input helped make this book a better publication.

We also express our appreciation to the numerous readers who were willing to share their expertise and knowledge on the subject of grief and funeral planning. Among them are: Marilyn Adams, Camarillo (CA) Hospice, John Buchanan, President, Continental Funeral and Memorial Society, Patrick Burke, Barbara Cleaver, co-founder of Mothers of Aids Patients (MAP), Janice Harris Lord, Director of Victims Services for Mothers Against Drunk Driving (MADD), Dr. Doyle Shields, Reverend Richard Weston-Jones, and Kathy Walczak, National Funeral Directors Association.

Special thanks to Dave Fischer for his cover design.

Martin Flagg expresses his personal appreciation to: Mike, for being there when we all needed you; to my mother, and to my wife, Nicole, my son, Nikolas, and to Grandfather Flagg.

Finally, our special acknowledgement goes to the publisher, Eugene D. Wheeler, without whose efforts and expertise *Final Celebrations* could not have been published.

CONTENTS

INTRODUCTION

Over 2.1 million Americans died in 1990, some naturally, others suddenly and unexpectedly. Countless numbers left no will or funeral instructions. To many, death is still a subject that one does not discuss or prepare for. As a result, survivors are left in grief scrambling about trying to plan a funeral, without knowing what the deceased wanted in the way of a burial and ceremony. At a stressful time, they are forced to make many important decisions. It's time for death to come out of the closet.

This book is about taking charge of the final celebration of life: the funeral ceremony of a loved one, or your own. It's wise to plan for one's funeral, as one would plan for a trip, or a major project. Funerals cost a lot of money, averaging as much as 5000 dollars in the United States, not including cemetery arrangements. Making these decisions when not under pressure can save families acrimony and money. This book will help you plan your final celebration and make intelligent decisions in the process through the options offered.

Final Celebrations **is for:**

- You who are prepared or want to be prepared for your own death.

- You who want to be prepared for a loved one's death, including:

    1. Loved ones who are ready to plan for the end of their lives.

2. Those who are terminally ill and need help in facing and preparing for death.

3. Those resisting the inevitability of death and not ready to look ahead.

- Survivors of an unexpected, sudden, or unprepared for death.
- Counselors, clergypersons, or persons having some other role in the helping professions, and
- For everyone because we're all going to die someday.

Being Prepared for Your Own Death

Final Celebrations is for you who are facing your own mortality and need a planning guide for the end of your life, how you want arrangements made for the disposal of your possessions and your body, and your memorial service. Planning for these final significant events, taking care of your unfinished business, and reaching closure is a gift to your friends and relatives.

Whether you want a traditional funeral, a memorial service, bequeathal of your body to a medical school, a private cremation with your ashes scattered, or no service at all is your individual choice. Reading the guidelines in these chapters will help you make and implement your decisions.

Being Prepared for a Loved One's Death

If a member of your family, a relative, or friend who is near death but is still in denial, this book may help you to invite discussion about this sensitive subject. It is for all of you who want to help, but don't know what to say and do to help your loved one to accept death as part of life, and find meaningful and deeply satisfying ways to celebrate the finality.

Loved One Is Ready to Plan for his Death

Perhaps your friend or relative is ready to involve himself in planning for death. You and he will find invaluable guidelines for the myriad decisions that will have to be made in the following chapters.

Those Resisting the Inevitability of Death

This book will help you with an elderly or terminally ill loved one who is having trouble facing the inevitability of the end of life. Facing one's mortality can mean going through the stages of grief that Elizabeth Kubler-Ross spelled out for bereavement: the shock of realization, denial (it can't happen to me), anger (why is everyone pushing me to talk about this gloomy subject?), depression (what's the use, I'm going to die anyway), and finally an acceptance of reality. This is not the same as resignation, which is a giving up and a giving in to a victim role. Acceptance is an act of the will, a saying yes to the inevitable and a willingness to move on.

Survivors of an Unexpected Death

In cases of sudden, unexpected, unprepared for death, this book can serve as an essential handbook to help you and the other people who were close to the deceased find your way through a labyrinth of unknown procedures involving emotional, financial, legal, and other issues.

Counselors and Helping Professionals

Counselors, ministers, doctors, lawyers, funeral directors, and others in the helping professions can use this book as adjunctive therapy, a tool to help their patients, parishioners, and clients deal with the immediate pressures and short-term and long-term decisions that are facing them.

For Everyone

And, finally, this book is for everyone. Planning our "Final Celebration" is partly for us, but mostly for our loved ones, the survivors, who are left with the pain and responsibility that this book will help us share with them.

Final Celebrations is intended to be a practical guide. It is not a study of grief. Many other quality books, like *No Time For Goodbyes,* by Janice Harris Lord, offer thorough, in-depth studies of the specific types of grief. A list of references is included in the Resources section. Death is as much a part of life as birth. Each of us is born into life a unique and special individual. When we die, the chain of humanity suffers the loss of that individual. A funeral or memorial service offers recognition and respect and is part of the final life process. Planning for it requires wisdom, courage, and boldness. But the reward, peace of mind, makes adequate preparation worth the effort. Assets are preserved, distributed according to the wishes of the deceased, and, most important, family dissension is avoided.

Every society throughout the ages has developed distinctive rituals for their dead. The information in this book will help you consider the many different burial and cremation services that exist in our society today. In each case, society's method of caring for the dead with ceremonies and rituals is an attempt to integrate death into the lives of those who remain. It is a ceremony to recognize the person's uniqueness, and to show respect for his or her contributions to life.

Much literature has been published on the dying process, how to prepare for it and how to cope with the inevitable that each of us will someday face. Grassroots self-help organizations such as Parents of Murdered Children, Compassionate Friends, and Mothers Against Drunk Driving provide help, hope, and support for survivors. The Resources Section of this book will introduce you to many such groups.

Just as you plan the life processes of birth, education, career, marriage and retirement, so, too, you can consider planning for your funeral. Why let fear prevent you from taking control of the final process?

Knowing you have taken care of these matters will leave you and your family with a certain peace of mind. It will not take the grief away, but it will allow you time to focus on healthy mourning. Taking creative control of the end of your life and helping loved ones do the same is a great challenge, the ultimate and final gift to yourself and your loved ones.

Editor's Note

Please note that in place of saying his or her, his is meant to refer to both sexes.

Copies of certain forms in Chapters One and Four are located at the end of the book and can be detached for personal use.

NOTES

CHAPTER 1

BEING PREPARED FOR YOUR OWN DEATH

> . . . To everything there is a season,
> A time for every matter under heaven:
> A time to be born, and a time to die...
>
> — Ecclesiastes 3:

VERONICA

Veronica, an Irish immigrant to America in the early 1900s, suffered from Alzheimer's disease for twelve years prior to her death. She had once been a vibrant, intelligent and successful businesswoman who raised two children alone after the early death of her husband. Her passing was peaceful and her final arrangements had been pre-planned because of the long illness. Her children wished to respect her Catholic background when planning the details of her funeral and also wanted to celebrate the things that had meant much to her in life. The service began in a traditional way with a visitation (rosary) held prior to the funeral. The priest explained to those attending the service the history of why the rosary is a tradition of the Catholic Church.

A young friend, now a Catholic priest, who had known Veronica all his life, drove 200 miles to say the funeral Mass and deliver a touching eulogy about Veronica's life. He remembered the positive and happy times she had shared with those present, the ways in which she had helped so many people, and he reassured the family that she was destined to be reunited with her family of 12 brothers and sisters in death. The priest even shared with Veronica's son the great pleasure he had derived from the musical instruments Veronica had given him. A memorial card was printed with an old Irish blessing. "May the road rise up to meet you, May the wind be always at your back......Until we meet again, May God hold you in the hollow of His hand."

The priest also sang her favorite hymns, "Ave Maria" and "Panis Angelicus," accompanied by an organist during the service. Her daughter prepared a special memorial essay with quotations from George Washington Carver and readings from one of Veronica's favorite authors, Ralph Waldo Emerson, "To laugh often and much; to win the respect of intelligent people and the affection of children...to know one life has breathed easier because you have lived. This is to have succeeded."

Finally, at the graveside ceremony, the priest sang Veronica's favorite song, "Danny Boy," accompanying himself on the guitar. The service was a combination of the traditional Catholic liturgical rites and a contemporary celebration relating to the deceased's background. The added personal readings and songs left family and mourners with warm memories of a woman who had touched their lives in a joyful and positive way.

AMANDA

Amanda's father, Professor Tate, had spent a quiet morning teaching at the University. He was particularly happy because she had phoned from England to tell him she had been accepted to participate in a special doctoral program at Oxford University. When the department secretary brought in a telegram from London during the lunch hour, a terrible fear crossed his mind as he peeled the yellow envelope open. "Regret to inform you......Amanda Tate has been killed in an automobile accident this AM... Please advise your plans."

In shock and grief, the professor and his wife were forced to make some of the most painful decisions of their lives. Should Amanda be cremated and then returned home? They remembered she didn't want to be cremated. She had expressed a desire to be buried in their hometown. After discussing it with his wife, Professor Tate set out on a bleak, lonely and expensive trip. He was forced to make many detailed decisions over the phone in order to return his daughter's body home. A quiet church service for family and friends was performed and Amanda was buried in the local cemetery.

These are two examples of a loved one's death, one planned for and one sudden and completely unexpected. Much of the Tate's confusion and distress could have been avoided if Amanda had made her funeral wishes known. All of us will someday be in the situation of handling the death of a loved one, a parent or grandparent, a child or a good friend. Are you prepared? Will you know what to do in such situations?

First Steps

Beyond planning the final celebration, consideration for surviving loved ones calls for you to write a will, indicating how you want your assets disposed of and other crucial matters. Anticipating your own death and making your last wishes known allows you to take control, to write your own epitaph. It lets others know of your most personal feelings and wishes. It helps your loved ones to remember you and the things you cared most about in life. It can be satisfying to select the recipients of your treasured items, furniture, jewelry, money, and books that you want your loved ones to have.

Not to indicate your desires for the disposal of your worldly goods and your body, and what you want for the ritual of your funeral leaves survivors in a quandary. Sometimes this can lead to bitter disagreement among family members over details of the funeral. Following is a list of practical information offered as a guideline to assist anyone with the myriad decisions involved in making last arrangements.

PERSONAL DATA TO BE KEPT AVAILABLE

Certain information should be kept documented in a place that family members know about and have easy access to. A safe deposit box often cannot be accessed immediately so it is not recommended that these papers be kept there. The information should include your name, date and place of birth, social security number, date and place of marriage, names and addresses of family members (brothers, sisters, children, grandchildren). If you are a veteran, you should keep your date of enlistment and discharge papers or photocopies in the same location.

If you have made prearrangements, let your loved one know where all the paperwork is kept. If not, prepare a form with the information listed below and let your loved ones know where it is located. At the end of this book, the following forms can be detached and added to your personal papers.

INSTRUCTIONS TO FOLLOW UPON MY DEATH

Pre-arrangement Information

I have prepared the following information to assist my loved ones in handling my final arrangements. Please follow through with what I have written. Do not change any of my last wishes unless the changes cannot be avoided. Thank you.

Personal Information

Name_____ Date _____

Address _____

_____

City_____State _____

Social Security No.: _____

Date of Birth: _____

Place of Birth:_____

Date of Marriage: _____

Place of Marriage: _____

Father's name and birthplace (addresses and telephone numbers if living): _____

_____

Mother's name and birthplace (addresses and telephone numbers if living): _____

_____

Major places and number of years of residence:

Locally: _____

Other: _____

_____

Education, list and dates of degrees received:

High School: _____

College:_____

Post Graduate: _____

Other: _____

Work Experience: _____

_____

Employer: _____

Job Title: _____

From (Date):_____To (Date): _____

Date of Retirement: _____

Veteran Information:

Branch of Service: _____

Wars Served: _____

Medals or Special Service:_____

_____

Place and Date Entered Service: _____

Date of Discharge: _____

Rank and Serial Number: _____

Organization or outfit:_____

Location of discharge papers: _____

Flag desired to drape casket: Yes: No:

Religious Affiliation:

Religion: _____

Church Affiliation: _____

Professional or Fraternal organizations:

_____

_____

Other Organizations/Special Interests: _____

_____

Remarks: _____

_____

Funeral Arrangements

Autopsy Permission

Name_____

I will permit autopsy (unless authorities require it).

___Yes ___No

Relatives and Friends to Notify
(Names, addresses, and telephone numbers)
Survivors:
Spouse: _____

Other: _____

Parents: _____

_____

Children: _____

_____

Brothers: _____

_____

Sisters: _____

_____

Names, addresses and telephone numbers of friends to notify:

_____

_____

Number of Nieces: _____   Number of Nephews:_____
Number of Grandchildren: _____
Number of Great-Grandchildren:_____
Donations to be made in my memory: _____

_____

Pallbearers I would like: _____

_____

_____

Honorary Pallbearers: _____

_____

_____

Others to notify of my death: _____

_____

Any additional instructions or considerations not included in
the list above: _____

_____

Location of Important Information, Papers, and Documents

Name _____

Location of will: _____

The name , address, and telephone number of legal advisor: _

_____

Location of safety deposit box and key: _____

_____

Bank trust department: _____

_____

Location of all checking and savings accounts (address and branch No., Acct. No.): _____

_____

_____

Location of checkbooks and passbooks: _____

_____

Credit cards and charge accounts to be cancelled: _____

_____

Location of insurance policies: _____

_____

Location of Service Discharge Papers:_____

_____

Trusts in effect: _____

_____

Insurance policies: _____

_____

Power of Attorney, funeral pre-arrangements if made: _____

_____

_____

My Executor/Executrix is: _____

_____

My Physician is: _____

_____

Living Will: _____

_____

Durable Power of Attorney for Health Care: _____

_____

In addition to basic personal data, you or your loved ones should leave other information to help your family. Be sure to leave a summary of your achievements and the groups you have been involved with. What type of service would you like? What type of music? Do you have favorite songs you would like to be played or sung at your funeral? Any special readings or poetry? Is there a certain individual you would like to give a Eulogy? A sample Pre-arrangement Form to use as a guide follows.

PRE-ARRANGED FUNERAL SERVICE INFORMATION

Name_____

My Service is to be held at: _____

Clergy: _____

Church, Funeral Home, or special place: _____

Special Music: _____

_____

Organist/Other: _____

_____

I would like the eulogy said by: _____

_____

I wish to be cremated (See separate Cremation form):_____

Visitation location and time: _____

Casket should be open: _____closed: _____

Casket I prefer: _____

_____

Outer enclosure (vault) I prefer: _____

_____

Cemetery to be used and instructions: _____

_____

Cemetery lot: Section: _____

Lot:_____Block:_____Space: _____

Committal at grave side: _____

Clothing to use: _____

_____

Jewelry I wish to wear: _____

_____

Instructions for disposition of jewelry before burial: _____

_____

Flowers or Memorial Donation: _____

Other special instructions: _____

_____

Death with Dignity

In addition to making personal information available, you want to consider other legal documents. More and more individuals abhor the idea of being kept alive on machines when there is no chance of recovery. They would prefer a death with more dignity. Because some would prefer to be in control at the end of life, "right to die" movements have sprung up throughout the United States, Canada, Europe, and other countries. Doctors and hospitals in our society are focused on keeping people alive. For this reason it is important that you discuss with your family what your wishes are, and fill out a Living Will and a Durable Power of Attorney For Health Care. Copies should be given to your family, your physician, your attorney, and the hospital if you are admitted with a terminal illness. Keep these documents in a safe place with your will and other estate planning information. Let your family or loved ones know where they are stored.

To date, the Natural Death Act has been enacted in 13 states and Washington, D.C., and the Durable Power of Attorney (but not for Health Care) is authorized in 42 states. You can research your state laws through local memorial societies or funeral homes. There is growing awareness of people's wishes to die with dignity and doctors and hospitals are increasingly supporting the idea of not prolonging a terminally ill patient's life if the person does not want it himself.

New ballot initiatives have been proposed by "death with dignity" advocates in several states. More and more individuals are expressing their desire to take control of their last living act.

The Hemlock Society

The Hemlock Society is an educational organization which supports the option of active voluntary euthanasia or "self-deliverance" for the advanced, terminally ill mature adult, or the seriously, incurably physically ill person. This organization campaigns to bring better understanding of euthanasia to the public and to work towards improved laws. A quarterly newsletter with up-to-date legal, ethical, and operating developments is published. Their address is listed in the Resource Section.

The Living Will form can be obtained from Choice In Dying, Inc. (listed in the Resource Section). Durable Power of Attorney for Health Care forms are available wherever legal forms are sold. A Living Will combined with a Durable Power of Attorney for Health Care form can be obtained from the National Hemlock Society, P.O. Box 11830, Eugene, OR 97440-3900.

LEGAL DOCUMENTS TO CONSIDER

Wills and Trusts

Everyone should have a will to dispose of his assets. Many choose to also set up a revocable trust with their legal advisor to avoid probate. These documents should be placed in a safe but accessible location for family members. It is not recommended they be kept in a safe deposit box. If no will exists, state law will determine who inherits the estate. It is advised that families read wills prior to the funeral service to understand the deceased's last wishes. Often, they wait until after the funeral and miss something asked for in the will.

Living Wills

Living Wills are documents signed by individuals who are still mentally healthy, which make known their wishes about prolonging treatment at the time of death. It instructs one's doctor, family and friends of the individual's desires concerning the use of heroic measures or artificial means (machines) to prolong life. Effective in December, 1991, medical institutions in the United States must document, upon admission, whether patients have made out a living will and whether they have appointed a surrogate decision-maker. The procedure is part of the Patient Self-Determination Act, a Medicare amendment that was passed in the 1990 federal budget bill. It reaffirms Americans' right to control decisions about medical treatments. Congress recommends that citizens write down their preferences in advance.

Durable Power Of Attorney For Health Care

The Durable Power of Attorney For Health Care is a legal document giving someone else legal authority to make the decision whether to continue to provide certain medical treatment in a terminal illness if the patient is unconscious or unable to make the decision himself.

After executing the necessary legal documents you can consider alternative methods of funeral planning. You can obtain information from a local non-profit memorial society or your local funeral home. Listed below is information on these topics to assist you.

HELPFUL ORGANIZATIONS

Memorial Societies

Memorial Societies are non-profit, consumer based, cooperative organizations started by churches, individuals, and organizations to aid people seeking simple and dignified funerals at reasonable prices. They do not offer funeral services, but act in an advisory capacity and sometimes work in conjunction with funeral directors. They provide information about what to do when death occurs and offer a choice of simple and dignified alternatives. Many work with funeral directors who are willing to provide services for moderate prices. The societies offer information on legal requirements, death benefits and other related topics. Members can choose the plan they prefer and make their wishes known to the society, the funeral home, and their family.

Memorial societies vary in their arrangements and operation. Commonly, they are democratic and non-profit. There are other societies that provide services, such as cremation, for profit. If you wish to verify that you are dealing with a genuine non-profit memorial society, check to see if it is a member of the Continental Association of Funeral & Memorial Societies (address located in Resource Section). Most in the U.S. are members of this association, which screens its members carefully. Bona fide societies have no commercial interests and membership is relatively inexpensive.

Memorial societies began in the northwestern United States in the early 1900s with the Farm Grange organization. Societies now exist in over 200 North American cities and in Canada.

Most of the societies in the U.S. and Canada are members of the Continental Association. Anyone can join for a one time fee, usually in the $10 to $30 range. Advance funeral planning can be done and does not involve advance payment of funeral costs. The societies work to insure that an individual's plans are carried out as stated, and allow these plans to be changed or canceled at any time. They can offer great assistance to the family of the deceased coordinating arrangements and relieving stress for the survivors. Membership is usually transferable to a new geographic region if you relocate.

Funeral Associations

The National Funeral Directors Association is an organization of licensed funeral directors and funeral homes dedicated to the highest standards of funeral service. They offer help with many facets of the funeral industry and can answer questions about funeral homes in your area.

The International Order of the Golden Rule is an international association of independent funeral homes in which membership is by invitation only. In addition to these, there are other professional organizations listed in the Resource Section.

The American Cemetery Association is an organization of cemetery professionals that can help with questions pertaining to cemetery matters, or direct you to a cemetery in your area. The address is in the Resource Section.

The Cremation Association of North America (CANA) is an association of crematories, cemeteries, and funeral homes that offer cremation. More than 600 members belong who own and operate crematories and who encourage the concept of memorialization (see the Resource Section).

For a free directory of funeral and memorial societies and a list of additional publications, write the Continental Association of Funeral and Memorial Societies, Inc. (CAFMS), 33 University Square, Suite 333, Madison, WI. 53715 - telephone (800) 458-5563. A partial list of societies is provided in the Resource Section.

The Role of the Funeral Home and Staff

It takes a particular type of individual to fulfill the funeral director's many roles. Good funeral directors are caring people who enjoy working with others. They are required to fulfill certain educational requirements, the minimum being high school graduation, some college, and at least one year of professional curriculum. Programs include courses in chemistry, sociology, psychology, and public health. Many take courses in embalming and bacteriology as well. After professional courses are completed, all states require the student to pass a state board or national licensing examination. Requirements vary from state to state.

A death in any family burdens survivors with grief and disrupts their normal schedule. When a funeral home is called after a person dies, the staff has many tasks to perform. The initial responsibility is to bring the deceased's body to the funeral home. Arrangements must be made to transport the individual, perhaps even from out of state. The necessary information for the death certificate and other legal requirements are handled.

The funeral home staff will meet with the family and discuss their plans for cremation, burial in the ground, or bequeathal of body, and a service. According to the family's wishes, the staff helps them make choices that will meet their needs, the type of service desired, visitation, the vault and casket, permission to embalm, the type of burial, the grave marker, and other items as necessary. If pre-arrangements have been made, the staff will go over them in detail with family members. In addition, the staff will attend to ceremonial and administrative details of the funeral. They will inform the family of the benefits available such as Social Security or Veteran's benefits.

Today's funeral directors and their staffs are trained to help families cope with death. Some funeral homes sponsor grief recovery programs. Most funeral directors spend long hours providing a service for others in a time of need.

As you can see, a funeral can require a lot of decisions. Planning ahead can reduce the headaches to survivors.

TYPES OF CEREMONIES

Once you have decided on a funeral home or memorial society, the next step is to choose the type and location of the service or ceremony you wish. There are basically three types of death ceremonies practiced in our society: funeral, committal or commitment, and memorial. In addition, today more people wish to plan a unique service of their own. No set rules exist.

Funeral Service

A funeral service is a ceremony held with the body present in either a closed or open casket, depending on the wishes of the deceased and family members. The ceremony can be traditional like those performed by religious groups such as the Catholic, Protestant, Jewish, or other faiths. The service can also be a combination of a memorial service and traditional ceremonies. The desires of the deceased and the family prevail. Self-planned services can take many forms. Sometimes the family and friends will meet in a home for an evening to discuss and remember a loved one. Some prefer conventional services with songs, readings and perhaps one or more special individuals delivering a eulogy for the deceased. All this can be outlined by the individual in pre-planning.

If someone wishes, multiple services can be held. For example, a ceremony in the area where the person died and later in his home town which might be in another state. This allows friends to commemorate his life.

In the case of a miscarriage or the death of a very young child, families often hold a small private service in which they name the child and celebrate the birth and death. Such a memorial helps the grieving process.

A recent service that can be provided through funeral directors by the National Music Service, Inc. is a video presentation of a life remembered. The company prepares video biographies using slides and pictures of the deceased (or for pre-planned services) which can be presented at the ceremony and kept as a memento by the family after the service. Your funeral director can provide more information. (See the Resource Section).

Committal Service

A committal service is a brief, optional service held at the gravesite, in a chapel of a crematorium, or a cemetery chapel. Often used in combination with a funeral or memorial service, it is an occasion where the immediate family, close friends and loved ones gather to bid goodbye to the deceased.

Memorial Service

A memorial service is a service held without the body of the deceased present. Perhaps the death occurred somewhere else and now the survivors in the deceased's home wish to commemorate the individual. Some people desire cremation immediately after death and a memorial service held afterward. Cremains are sometimes present if desired. The service can be held at any time to accommodate the needs of the family members. It does not have to take place soon after a death occurs, but can be planned one, two, or several weeks later. The mood of memorial services is usually a positive one and family participation is encouraged. Individuals are often asked, never coerced, to tell something they remember about the deceased.

Time and Location of Service

Services are usually planned to take place a few days after the death and can be held in any appropriate place. In some cases families hold memorial services two or three weeks later after having the deceased cremated in order to allow friends and relatives in other parts of the country time to make personal and travel arrangements to attend. Some prefer to hold a small service outdoors, others desire a gathering in a chapel, synagogue, or church. With planning, you can make your desires known.

In all ceremonies, flexibility is possible. You may write down whatever your wishes are. Families need not be afraid to discuss different possibilities with clergy or a funeral home director. Some examples of funeral ceremonies are outlined in Chapter 7.

Once you have taken care of the necessary legal requirements, documented your personal data, and investigated your local memorial societies and/or funeral homes, the next step in preparing arrangements for yourself will be to decide on the method of final disposition you desire; burial, cremation or body bequeathal. These alternatives are discussed in more detail in Chapters 3, 4, and 5.

CHAPTER 2

BEING PREPARED FOR THE DEATH OF A LOVED ONE

...Grief is itself a medicine.

— William Cowper

When the death of a mate, friend or relative occurs, you may feel shocked or helpless. Planned funeral arrangements can help bring some peace of mind. If your loved one has not planned for a funeral and you are responsible for providing "*at need*" arrangements, (funeral arrangements that must be made immediately due to a sudden death), there are many clergypersons and other professional people, as well as your own close family members and friends, who can assist. An experienced funeral home staff is a valuable resource in a time of need. Remember, you need not be alone.

Families can ease the shock and confusion if they try to get a mate or elderly loved ones to prepare a funeral plan. The family should prepare an emergency plan for those close to them if a terminally ill person is reluctant to do so. Special circumstances arise in the cases of sudden or accidental death and the terminally ill. There are many organizations that can offer help.

SUDDEN OR ACCIDENTAL DEATH

A sudden or accidental death of a loved one is harder to handle than an expected death from natural causes. Survivors aren't ready and are left with nagging questions, words never to be spoken and wishes never expressed. Shock and disbelief may delay acceptance of the loss. The more unexpected the death, the harder it is to believe it has happened.

Sudden death can occur in many ways: murder, accident, heart attack, stroke, or the unexplainable sudden death of an infant. In every case, survivors are left in a state of shock and disbelief. Some collapse physically and others lash out violently at the bearer of the bad news.

The survivors may be forced to accept the fact that their loved one's body is mutilated, perhaps even beyond recognition as in the case of many auto or aircraft accidents. They may be asked to identify the deceased. If the accident was caused by negligence as in the case of drunk drivers, they may find it difficult to contain their initial anger.

Those who have lost loved ones to senseless violence, murder or accidental death may be forced to deal with the seemingly uncaring legal system. They may have to wait for years for justice to be carried out.

As the reality of the death begins to sink in, survivors will probably experience depression. They may feel that nothing matters any more. This is normal. They will need time to accept the loss and express their grief. Suggest that the survivors seek help from support groups like Mothers Against Drunk Drivers, Compassionate Friends, and Parents of Murdered Children (see the Resource Section). Be aware that each person grieves in his own time in his own way. If he is not coping, don't be afraid to suggest professional counseling.

When you lose a loved one, whether it is a spouse, a parent, a child, or close friend, you can feel very alone. You can't believe that this has happened. Along with denial, you may have anger. Depending on your age and personal living situation, in addition to the shock of losing a loved one, you may also experience secondary losses such as financial loss or the loss of a helping parent in the family. Whatever the circumstances, it is never easy to accept death. Certain types of death are particularly hard, such as Sudden Infant Death Syndrome (SIDS), violent or accidental death, or an untimely death from AIDS.

Death Of An Infant

When an infant dies before or shortly after birth, there is a special sadness and grief. Parents sometimes have difficulty saying goodbye to someone they had little chance to know. A mother may mourn the miscarriage of the fetus she carried in her womb in the same way she would grieve for that child had it lived through birth. Grandparents suffer a double burden, mourning the loss of a grandchild they will never get to know, and watching their own children grieve over that loss, too.

Sudden Infant Death Syndrome (SIDS)

An especially painful loss is the death of a baby or young child to Sudden Infant Death Syndrome (SIDS). Parents may experience great anger and guilt for the feeling that they weren't more vigilant. The guilt may deepen when a medical investigation required by county health officials is conducted. Parents may be overcome by a tremendous sense of emptiness. They may experience deep depression.

Some parents who lose infants before or shortly after birth, and especially parents of SIDS infants, want to hold a memorial service. Take time to decide exactly what you want to do. Spouses should decide together. Parents should consider joining a self-help group such as Source of Help in Airing and Resolving Experiences (SHARE), an association of bereaved parents, Compassionate Friends or other groups for parents who lose an infant. See the Resource Section for a list of support groups.

Death Of A Child

Loss of a child, teenager or young adult is also difficult. Most people expect to bury their parents someday when they grow elderly and die. The death of a young person is not in the natural order of life. It is difficult to accept. "The relationship between a parent and child is different from any other relationship in the world," says Dr. Therese Rando, a clinical psychologist and author of *Parental Loss of A Child.* "Parents who lose a child also lose the hopes, dreams, and expectations they had for that child. They lose parts of themselves. The child represents their sense of ongoing life." Your shock, denial, anger and guilt will be felt to a greater degree than normal if you lose a child.

Fred Rogers of the *Mr. Rogers Television Show* has written *So Much To Think About...When Someone You Care About Has Died* as an aid to help children understand death. It is compiled of stories, memory pages, pencil games, cards and other activities along with a simple text that accepts children's feelings and reactions to a death. A catalog of all the Mister Rogers' material for children and adults is available through Family Communications, listed in the Resource Section.

Suicide

It is often difficult for survivors to accept the loss of a loved one by suicide. Many can't understand what leads a person to end his own life. In cases where someone has a terminal illness or has suffered unrelenting pain, friends understand. But when a young person or someone in the prime of his life decides to end it, relatives and friends are left in a state of shock.

From 1960 to 1990, suicides in the United States increased by 11 percent. Suicide among adolescents tripled and in the early to mid '80s there was a 21 percent upturn in the incidence of suicide among the elderly.

Survivors of relatives or friends who have committed suicide should consider joining a self-help group such as Ray of Hope or Survivors of Suicide (See the Resource Section). They should seek professional counseling if their grief continues to overwhelm them for a long period of time.

Death Due to Drunk Driving

Another devastating form of sudden death is death due to drunk driving. In the United States more than 250,000 people were killed by drunk drivers in the past 10 years. In 1990, an estimated 22,415 persons died in alcohol-related traffic crashes, 49.2% of the 45,555 total traffic fatalities. These deaths, along with the hundreds of thousands of injuries, represent enormous pain and tragedy for the survivors.

Mothers Against Drunk Driving, a grassroots organization, was founded in 1980 by a group of concerned citizens, led by Candy Lightner, whose 13 year old daughter, Cari, was killed by a drunk driver while walking in a bicycle lane in Fair Oaks, California.

MADD's goals are to provide counseling and support for the victim families of drunk driving crashes; to raise public awareness about drinking and driving issues; to prevent illegal alcohol use by youth and educate them about the dangers of drinking and driving; and to change public policy about drinking and driving at the state and national level. MADD is dedicated to providing support for the families of these victims. Write or call your local chapter or the national office listed in the Resource Section for help and information.

THE TERMINALLY ILL

Another large segment of the population who need help in preparing for death and final celebrations are the terminally ill. Many of these people prefer to die at home rather than in some large institution or hospital.

Hospice

Many communities have established programs affiliated with hospitals and nursing care associations to assist patients who are dying from cancer and other terminal diseases and their families. These service organizations for the terminally ill provide much needed assistance and are well received by the ill and their families. They provide a humane alternative to costly hospitalization in large impersonal institutions.

Often, terminally ill people have no plans for their funeral and need to be approached about their last wishes. Many won't talk about their coming death. These situations make it difficult for survivors who must handle the final disposition of their loved one's personal belongings and resources. Speaking with a counselor or clergyperson may help you to prepare in this difficult situation. Often hospice volunteers can be of assistance.

The word hospice means a place of refuge. In the United States, the volunteer-staffed hospice service is a concept of care that focuses on enhancing the quality of life and meeting the special needs of those living with life-threatening illness and the needs of their families. Volunteers provide emotional support for the patients and their families during the period of illness and, later, to the surviving family and friends during the time of bereavement. Hospice groups aim to preserve the dignity and personal choices of each patient.

St. Christopher's Hospice, founded in London in 1967, has been a model for hospice programs in North America. A majority of these volunteer-staffed programs operate home care programs with no actual in-patient facility. Their goal is to provide alternative care for ill and dying persons. Receiving care in a home setting greatly helps dying patients and their families prepare emotionally for death. Most terminally ill people experience feelings of rejection from those around them in a large hospital institution. One of the greatest needs of the dying is the desire to talk about their life. When they are continually heard, accepted, and loved by their families, friends and care-givers, they learn to more easily accept their situation.

When death is near, some individuals may prefer silence or lapse into a coma. This is a natural reaction. Many people believed to be unconscious still hear what is being said around them. Quiet words of affection and love can give final comfort and warmth to the dying individual.

Most hospice organizations operate independently and offer service to patients and their families regardless of age, sex, religion, or financial status. For eligibility, a patient need only have a diagnosis commonly considered to be terminal or life-threatening, with a prognosis of approximately one year or less.

Some of the services provide liaison with physicians, home health agencies, and hospital staff that will assist the patient to remain pain free and comfortable in the hospital or at home, if this is practical and desirable. They also provide professional counseling to families to equip them to care for the patient at home and to help the patient deal with his illness and grief.

Volunteers provide friendly visiting and practical assistance such as transportation and errands, and provide respite to families, allowing them to leave the hospital or home setting for a time. They provide telephone assurance and a listening ear during the crises. Bereavement services and support groups are also offered following the death.

Under Medicare, hospice is primarily a home-care program which provides all necessary and reasonable medical and support services for the management of a terminal illness, including pain control. When the patient receives these services from a Medicare-certified hospice, Medicare hospital insurance pays almost the entire cost.

A patient can receive hospice care for two periods of 90 days each and one 30-day period – a lifetime maximum of 210 days. If hospice care is chosen and later the patient decides not to use it, he can cancel at any time and resume standard hospital and medical insurance benefits under Medicare Part A and Part B. Medicare pays hospice directly for the full cost with the exception of two items. The first is drugs or biologicals for pain relief in which case the hospice can charge 5 percent of the reasonable cost, up to a maximum of $5 for each outpatient prescription. The second is inpatient respite care which is care that offers relief to the primary caretaker. Hospice can charge 5 percent of the cost of the inpatient stay. Respite care is limited each time to stays of no more than five days in a row. More detail is outlined in *Your Medicare Handbook* available at any Social Security Office.

Most hospice organizations depend on donations from individuals and organizations, membership fees, grants, memorials, legacies and special fund-raising events. With the cost of health care increasing at an alarming rate, dying individuals can incur tremendous costs. The hospice organization provides an affordable alternative to these individuals and their families who otherwise have no choices. For information concerning hospice in your area, contact the National Hospice Organization listed in the Resource Section.

Acquired Immunodeficiency Syndrome (AIDS)

The tragedy of untimely death due to acquired immunodeficiency syndrome (AIDS) is especially sad. Many victims and their families feel a terrible grief, a hopelessness in the face of this plague. They have a great need for support in their grieving and are frequently abandoned.

The disease has polarized many groups against each other at a time when cooperation is sorely needed. There are reports about it every day in the newspapers and on television. "Talented young musician is struck down in his prime." "Schoolmates shun young child." "Family is forced to move from the community."

AIDS has spread to almost every country in the world and a research organization in London has predicted that in the next decade one million people in Africa will die of the disease. It is estimated that 5 to 10 million people in the world are already infected with the HIV virus and many have developed AIDS. One million or more cases could emerge in the next two years.

AIDS strikes down individuals in their prime. It has taken men, women, children, even infants. Many AIDS patients have courageously planned their own funerals. See Chapter 7 for the sample memorial service one 25 year old planned for himself.

Most morticians take precautions with all bodies and assume that each that died might have had a contagious disease. Morticians have no way of knowing of the medical history of a deceased person. Most funeral homes do not charge extra for dealing with the body of one who has died of AIDS or other contagious diseases. A funeral home or memorial society can provide more information. Groups that provide support for AIDS patients are listed in the Resource Section.

The Shanti Foundation

AIDS groups have established hospice-like organizations such as the Shanti Foundations in San Francisco and Los Angeles to aid and assist the terminally ill in their homes. Shanti, from a Sanskrit word for "inner peace through fuller understanding," provides compassion and understanding so that those facing the uncertainty of a life-threatening illness need not face it alone. Founded to provide emotional support to those facing the AIDS crisis, they have found that those with strong support systems actually live longer and enjoy a higher quality of life than those with limited support. Shanti now offers peer counseling for all those affected by life-threatening illness, including HIV/AIDS and cancer. The services are extended to families and significant others as well. They are led by trained facilitators and offer needed support. Shanti also sponsors a Special Health Education Program (SHEP) which presents monthly health seminars on HIV related issues and other education and support groups. Like hospice groups, Shanti relies on volunteers and donations for help and support. For more information, contact Shanti Foundation, listed in the Resource Section.

Summary

Each type of death presents its own unique challenges. Today, tragic illnesses like cancer, AIDS, and accidental or criminally violent deaths take the lives of many in an untimely way. New resources and approaches to the subject of death have appeared to address those victims. Death education is now offered on college campuses. An organization called Association for Death Education and Counseling now certifies professional grief educators and grief therapists. Hospice organizations assist the terminally ill and Child Bereavement Centers are springing up over the country.

STEPS TO TAKE WHEN A DEATH OCCURS

There are laws which vary from state to state, making it necessary for a doctor or nurse to be present and verify the death of a person, stating the cause. The funeral director will arrange to get a doctor's signature on the death certificate or contact the coroner's office if necessary. If there is doubt as to the cause or a question that the death is the result of homicide or suicide, the county coroner or medical examiner will be called.

Listed below is a brief summary of what happens and what action is called for by survivors in different situations when a death occurs.

Unexpected Death in the Home

If someone is stricken at home or in another non-medical setting, call your local paramedics or rescue squad. In many areas, you can obtain assistance by calling 911 or the operator. Even if you think your loved one has already died, it's best to call for assistance. At times, there may be a chance of revival. If the death is unquestionable, it's better to call the mortician, especially if final arrangements have been planned. A useless trip to a hospital can be costly. Call your family physician to confirm the death. Call the coroner and report the death if the paramedics don't. If the police are involved, the body may be taken to the coroner's office.

Death in the Home after an Illness

Call the attending physician or nursing agency to confirm the death. If a doctor has been in attendance, he may sign the death certificate.

Death Due to an Accident

The body normally will be taken to a coroner or hospital. Someone in authority must determine the cause of death for the death certificate.

Death in a Hospital

When death occurs in a hospital or other medical facility, a member of the staff will call the doctor of the deceased, or a hospital physician will determine the cause of death for the death certificate.

Death in a Nursing Home

If a doctor has been in attendance, he can usually determine the cause of death for the death certificate.

Death away from Home

If you are with the deceased at the time of death, notify the paramedics or coroner's office and get emergency help locally. You will need to notify the deceased's family or, if the person is your relative, your own. Do the same in the case of an accident after the authorities have removed the body. Be sure to find out where the body is to be taken. If funeral plans have been pre-arranged you can call that funeral home (at the deceased's home) and have them take care of arrangements in the city where the death occurred. They will contact a funeral home and take care of cremation, if called for in a plan, or embalming, and transporting the body or cremains home. If no pre-arrangements exist, a local funeral home can coordinate arrangements with your choice of a funeral home in the home location.

After release of the body by a coroner or doctor, the mortician of choice should be called. Staff members will be sent to remove the remains and obtain the necessary death certificate information. The mortician will arrange to have the doctor or coroner sign the completed death certificate.

If death occurs in a foreign country, call the American Embassy as soon as possible. They will assist in arrangements for shipment or for local disposition of the deceased.

CONTACTS TO MAKE AFTER A DEATH

Memorial Society or Funeral Home

If the deceased had selected a mortuary, you should contact them next. If not, a funeral home needs to be contacted. A member of a memorial society will usually carry a card giving mortuary details. One of the best ways to select a funeral home is by asking for references from family and friends, from the National Funeral Directors' Association, or from a local memorial society. The next step is to call the person's clergyperson. Let the funeral director know this information so schedules can be coordinated. Clergypersons want to be notified as soon as possible to allow time to plan and schedule a service. The funeral home and clergyperson can provide you with their schedule and let you know of their availability to conduct the service. The family and close friends of the deceased should be notified. After you have notified the immediate family, consider delegating further telephone calls.

By setting the plans for the deceased into motion, you are initiating your own grieving process too, by affirming the death in your own mind as you announce it to others.

This is a time when the immediate family comes under great strain. Thoughtful friends and relatives can help with many minor things like cooking, child care and shopping. You can help by actively assisting. Don't just say "If there's anything I can do...let me know." Some suggestions follow.

List of Helpful Actions to Assist Survivors

- Make a list of family and friends who need to be contacted. Make the calls.

- Make arrangements for members of the family or close friends to answer the telephone or the door.

- Arrange for child care if needed.

- Run any special errands needed.

- Help the family decide on flowers or a particular organization that they wish donations to be sent to. Let people know when you call.

- Coordinate shopping and the cooking of meals.

- Coordinate the food for any meeting to be held in the home after the service.
- Accompany the surviving family to the funeral home to help make arrangements.

NOTES

CHAPTER 3

FUNERAL AND BURIAL INFORMATION

...A covered bridge leading from light to
light through a brief darkness.
                — Henry Wadsworth Longfellow

In addition to preparing the information that will be needed at the time of your death and leaving your special wishes written for your family, you also may want to consider "pre-need" planning with your local funeral director or memorial society. This involves deciding on the purchase of a casket, vault, burial site, etc., if to be buried. If you wish to be cremated, other decisions need to be made; are cremains to be buried or scattered at sea? Will there be a service in a church or at the funeral home? Pre-need arrangements have increased tremendously during the last decade. Many families select and pre-pay for services, caskets, vaults, cemetery plots, simple cremation, or other special needs.

Of the 2,162,000 deaths in the United States in 1990, 1,794,000 or 82.9 percent, chose burial in the ground. It is significant to note that nationwide, 17.02% of Americans chose cremation in 1990. In California the figure was higher, 40.12%, and increasing. In Florida it was 34.46%. The interest in cremation in the United States has grown considerably over the previous decade.

Pre-planning allows individuals to make their own choices. They can thus take control and save their families the anguish of being faced with many important and expensive decisions when under the pressure of grief. An option is to prepare a plan for a funeral, but not to pre-pay. Your local memorial society or funeral director can assist you with this.

Autopsy

Autopsies are performed to determine the exact cause of death. Some diseases, like Alzheimer's Disease, cannot be positively identified until an autopsy is performed. In certain cases, the autopsy contributes to medical knowledge and research. A person can give permission for an autopsy to be performed after death, or leave instructions with the family as to his desires. Keep in mind that if medical authorities believe an autopsy is necessary, they will perform it despite the views of survivors. However, if you wish to donate a major organ to medical research, be careful about requesting an autopsy. Some medical schools will not accept body bequeathal when major organs are missing. In most cases, autopsy helps to improve the experience and knowledge of doctors and medical research. Make your wishes known concerning this procedure prior to your death.

Death Certificates And Obituaries

Having access to personal data of the deceased will allow the funeral director to procure a death certificate. This is a legal document that contains the deceased's historical information; date and cause of death, place of birth, place of death, social security number, parents, etc.

A certified death certificate is needed to finalize bank accounts, insurance policies, investments, and other aspects of an estate. Make a list of the various organizations before ordering copies. If the estate is a complicated one, you may need ten or twelve copies.

Sometimes procuring the death certificate may take longer than expected. If the death was of natural causes, it usually takes a few days. If the death was accidental, the result of crime, or the deceased did not have a physician in attendance to verify cause of death, the coroner or medical examiner may take charge of the case. This may cause a delay. At times, a temporary certificate is issued to allow the funeral director to proceed with the final disposition of the body. If you move to a new area, it is recommended that you transfer medical records to a new physician. This could help in preventing any delays in procuring a death certificate.

Obituaries

From the information provided in your personal data record, the funeral director will prepare an obituary notice for local newspapers. This will include statements about the history, birthplace, accomplishments of the deceased, club or military affiliations, and surviving relatives. The family may provide additional input, if desired, for newspapers. This is best done through the funeral home. Most newspapers have a specific format that they use when printing obituaries. Some newspapers charge a per line fee if the family wishes a special write-up or wants to include more information than the newspaper normally prints. Check with your local newspaper or funeral director for pricing details.

FUNERAL EQUIPMENT AND SERVICES

Caskets

The casket is the container in which the deceased is placed for the funeral service, for viewing, and for burial. However, some funeral homes have a program for rental of a casket for visitation purposes prior to cremation, if desired. The charge for a rental casket varies, but is around $600. Prices for caskets range from $395 to $8,000, but some cost as high as $20,000.

Caskets are made of several different materials: stainless steel, wood, copper, or bronze and marble. The quality and price of metal caskets are determined by the thickness of the metal. They are made with 20-gauge, 19-gauge, 18-gauge or 16-gauge steel. The lower gauge metal caskets are the thickest and of better quality. They are also more expensive due to the heavier metal content. Metal caskets come in a variety of colors and interiors. They can be protective or non-protective. Protective means that there is a rubber gasket around the base where the lid meets the top of the base. This gasket is meant to hinder the entrance of air, water and other outside materials into the casket. Non-protective metal caskets do not have this gasket and are closed by way of a snap-shut hinge located in the middle of the lid of the casket. Non-protective caskets are usually made with 20-gauge metal or higher.

Recently, stainless steel caskets have become in demand. Stainless steel caskets are not much more expensive than some 18-gauge or 16-gauge steel caskets. They come in a wide variety of colors and interiors.

Wood caskets are also used a lot. These are made from a variety of different wood such as cherry, oak, mahogany, walnut, poplar, and pine. Some caskets are also made of pressed wood and are referred to as "cloth covered" or "flat tops." These are the least expensive ranging in price from $300 to $700. As in other types, wood caskets come in different styles and colors of interiors. With unique wood grain patterns, no two wooden caskets are exactly alike. For this reason some people prefer them. Wooden caskets range from $1,200 to $4,000, but a quality mahogany casket can cost from $2,600 to $8,000.

Copper and bronze caskets are also in demand with some families. These caskets come in two finishes: brushed or smooth. They come in a wide variety of colors and interiors and have protective gaskets. Prices can range from $2,500 to $6,000.

Selecting a Casket

There is a lot more to selecting a particular casket than just color or eye appeal. When choosing a casket, check the interior, the handles, and the hardware. Some may have religious symbols in the head panel or other hardware which can be appealing. Most funeral directors excuse themselves from the casket selection room after answering any questions so the family can make a decision privately. If they don't, ask for privacy to make a family decision, if you wish. Take your time in selecting a casket suited for yourself, if you are making pre-arrangements, or for a member of your family or loved one who has died. Don't let a funeral director or pre-need specialist pressure you or a loved one into buying an item more expensive than you wish to pay. If you are pressured, you may want to consider using another firm. Even if a body is in one mortuary it can be moved to another one. You should feel comfortable with the appearance and the price of your selection.

Visitation

Visitation for the deceased is a scheduled time when an individual is presented for viewing in the casket so family, friends, and others can pay their last respects. Some religious ceremonies are combined with visitations such as a

Rosary being said for those of the Catholic faith. A casket, in some cases, can be obtained on a rental basis for those who desire a visitation prior to cremation. Your funeral director or memorial society can offer guidance as to the type of visitation and the length.

Viewing of the body of the deceased is a common custom in America. Many ancient cultures did this also. Critics believe that the practice is designed to provide more profit to funeral parlors, but others feel that it is a needed service offered to the mourners. Some consider it an important step in the grieving process. Viewing the body can allow survivors to begin the process of accepting the reality of death. A few religions, Judaism for example, frown on an open casket. Some religions believe it is better to remember the person as in life, rather than to have the dead body as a final image. Others believe it is healthy to view the deceased. Discuss it among your family members and with your clergyperson if you cannot decide.

Burial Garments

Another decision that must be made when planning a funeral is how to dress your loved one. If pre-planning was completed, this may have been decided. Most people want to be buried in garments that are typical of the "dress up" clothes an individual would wear when going out. Shoes are optional. You should include underwear, stockings or nylons, jewelry (if desired). Whatever your loved one is accustomed to wearing in everyday life is appropriate. You may want to consider the clothing appropriate to the deceased's condition. For example, one woman used a high collared dress to bury her mother because she had been ill and had lost so much weight. Another, a grieving mother, chose long sleeves for her son who had been on life support machines prior to his death and had many scars on his arms.

Be sure to bring dentures prior to embalming if the deceased wore them. They will help the mortician prepare the body in an appropriate and natural looking manner for viewing. Eye glasses are also important and should be brought to the funeral home. If the deceased wore them everyday in life, the person may feel they want to be buried with them on.

For young infants, you may want to include a receiving blanket or a nightgown or special bonnet. If the garment is unusual, you may want to leave instructions as to how to dress the infant. Again, it depends on the last wishes of the family.

Most funeral homes also have suits (ties are optional) and gowns to select from, but most people find that using the deceased's own clothing adds a personal touch. If you are pre-arranging your own funeral, let your loved ones know what you want to be buried in and where the garment is located. In the case of a terminally ill patient, the garments should be dry cleaned and wrapped, ready for use.

Vaults

The burial vault is an outer enclosure that the casket fits into as a container. Almost every cemetery requires the purchase of a vault to keep the ground from sinking into the gravesite after burial. There are two basic types of vaults; reinforced concrete or concrete grave liners (grave box). This is a simple concrete box and the least expensive. The most common burial vault is made of reinforced concrete. The price varies according to the material used in construction and weight. Vaults can range in cost from $195 to $2,000. A simple concrete grave box can cost from $200 to $400. A steel vault can range in price from $1,000 to $4,000. The grave box has no sealing function. Most cemeteries require an outer container. Check the requirements when you call the cemetery.

Basically, vaults are designed to stabilize the grave and provide peace of mind to a family. There is no way to prevent the eventual decomposition of human remains.

Embalming - What is it? Is it Necessary?

Embalming, while usually not required by law, is performed on a large percentage of bodies to be buried. If a visitation service with the body present is planned, embalming is normally necessary. It is a preservation process that dates back to the Egyptians who initiated it. Embalming briefly retards the decomposition of the body. The process gives family members or others time to think carefully about final disposition of the remains. If the body is intact, meaning the body didn't suffer from a disfiguring accident or illness, the process is relatively simple. If a body is to be cremated shortly after death, embalming is normally not necessary.

Embalming is the removal of blood from the deceased and replacing it with a solution that will preserve the body. An untreated body begins to decompose almost immediately. Embalming retards this process. Basically, the body's proteins are converted from a liquid state to a gel state which retards bacteria growth.

The embalmer will dress the body and apply cosmetics that are appropriate for the age and sex of the deceased. Those experienced in embalming can use some restorative methods, such as rebuilding sunken features or replacing missing hair if desired.

Embalming is performed by a licensed professional, either the funeral director or a licensed embalmer. All 50 states require licensure. Embalming is not routinely required, but will be if death was caused by a reportable contagious disease, if the remains are to be transported from one state to another, or if viewing the body is desired. Refrigeration can be used in place of embalming if a body is to be held for several days. It is normally cheaper than embalming. Some states require embalming if the body is to be moved at all. A funeral home or memorial society can inform you of the laws in your state. Directors are required to ask permission to embalm unless instructed otherwise by a health official. They may not charge a fee for unauthorized embalming unless it is required by state law.

CHOOSING A BURIAL SITE OR CEMETERY

Check cemetery prices and regulations by phone or visit the cemetery office to get the correct information on plot prices, fees, and charges in connection with vaults. While federal rules require funeral directors to disclose prices in advance, cemeteries are exempt from these laws.

Additional charges generally include the price of opening and closing the grave ($225 - $1525), installation of the marker on the grave ($125 - $1300), a slot for a vase on the marker and sales taxes.

Some choose burial in a crypt which is a concrete chamber in a mausoleum into which a casket is placed. Whenever available, a mausoleum, which is a building for the entombment of the dead, is a consideration. Prices vary in range depending on the wishes of an individual or their family.

If planning ahead, you can arrange to purchase a cemetery plot or mausoleum in advance. But be cautious. If a family should move, it will be difficult to sell a plot without taking a loss in the transaction. Call or visit the cemetery and get specific information, such as costs, and whether they permit headstones, or require ground-level markers. Also ask if they require grave liners or vaults, if they sell such items or charge for installation if you purchase them elsewhere. Check on the fees for opening and closing a grave, and on the cost of perpetual, or endowment care, i.e., maintenance of the gravesite.

Burial At Sea

Some funeral homes, in association with charter boats in both the Atlantic and Pacific oceans, now offer burial at sea services for anyone who chooses it. You do not have to be a Veteran. Ceremonies can be performed prior to burial at the funeral home or church, or on a chartered boat if desired. For burial at sea, embalming is usually required. The body is placed in a wooden box or casket which is weighted so it will sink. The Coast Guard requires that burial at sea be done in water which is at least 600 feet deep and approximately 60 miles out to sea. Costs for the burial at sea only (this does not include other items) range from $2500 to $4000.

Out of State Deaths

A person may wish to arrange for burial in a state other than the one in which he or she now resides. In such a case, two funeral homes will be involved, the forwarding funeral home and the receiving funeral home. The receiving home is usually known to your local director or selected from members of professional funeral organizations such as the National Funeral Directors Association or the International Order of the Golden Rule. The forwarding home (in the state in which the death occurs) will be the one to prepare the body, coordinate the legal paperwork and make flight or ground transportation arrangements. They work closely with the receiving home. The forwarding home handles details with the deceased's family in most cases, answering any questions they may have. The coordinating charges of both the forwarding and receiving funeral homes will range between $1,200 and $1,600, plus the actual shipping costs, when out of state funerals are coordinated.

Most major airlines offer "Grieving Fares" to immediate family members. The discounts range from 20 percent to 60 percent off normal prices. If a family member wishes to "escort" the remains on the same flight, this can be arranged. The remains will be shipped in the cargo area of the airplane and will require embalming for preservation purposes. A permit to bury should accompany the body. The receiving funeral home will be on hand at the destination to finalize the burial plans and assist the family with transportation and other needs. They will hold a visitation if the family desires. If no surviving family wishes to accompany the deceased or there are no living relatives, the receiving funeral home will handle the burial as arranged.

Delayed Burial

In some instances, burial may have to be delayed due to inclement weather or a scheduling conflict. This can be psychologically detrimental. Often, severe storms or the freezing of burial ground hinder the grave opening for burial. Many psychologists suggest this may cause a delay in the grieving process and recommend that when the final burial is made, a committal service at the burial site be held to help the grieving process. You may also want to consider a graveside committal service rather than holding a service in the chapel of a cemetery for this reason. You may need to use the cemetery chapel due to inclement weather, but it is recommended that you also go to the gravesite. This helps survivors deal with the finality of death and shows friends and relatives where the grave is located.

NOTES

Chapter 4

CREMATION

. . .Death is the sable smoke where vanishes the flame.

— Lord Byron

Cremation (incineration of the remains) is an increasingly used alternative to burial in the earth. Of the 2,162,100 deaths in the United States in 1990, the Cremation Association of North America reported that 367,975 or 17% were cremated. The deceased's body is taken in a casket or alternative container such as a cardboard box to a crematory where it is placed in a retort — a specially designed furnace — in which intense heat or fire reduces the body to a few pounds of bone fragments and ashes in about two hours. Smoke and gases from the furnace are recirculated so they don't escape into the open air. Bone ash is collected in a special area below the cremation chamber. Afterward, the bone and ashes are placed in an urn or canister which is then given to the relatives of the deceased or disposed of in a pre-designated way, such as scattering at sea, in a garden, or buried in the ground.

Some people prefer to keep the cremains in their homes in a special place. In addition to crematoriums and traditional funeral homes, there are memorial societies that will assist with the disposal of cremated remains (see the Resource Section).

Disposition of Cremains

The cremains, as these ashes are called, can be disposed of in many different ways. Laws governing this disposal vary from state to state. Families may choose to place the cremains in an urn and bury them in a grave or place them in a niche in a columbarium in a cemetery. A memorial headstone may be erected if so desired at a gravesite or at a place of burial. In the United States some have a tree planted in a memorial garden over the spot where their cremains are buried.

Regulations of most crematories require that the remains of the deceased be placed in a container of rigid construction. Others may prefer that their cremains be scattered over the ocean, in a river, or stream or over the ground. In California, it is forbidden to scatter cremains over land. Many leave special instructions in their pre-arrangement plans. For example, some people request that the formerly cremated ashes of a beloved pet be mixed or buried with their own. Some locations do not legally allow scattering of cremains, so you should ask for advice from a funeral director or memorial society about restrictions.

The urns used to house the cremains come in wood, marble, pewter, a combination of bronze and wood or other metals. Costs range from under $100 to more than $1,000. The cremains are returned to the funeral home from the crematory in a plastic box inside a cardboard box, along with a certificate of cremation. Some cemeteries will allow burial in this plastic box, others will not. Some cemeteries and states require a particular strength container for burial of cremains. Some states like California permit next-of-kin to keep the cremains at home. Again,

you should check what the legal and procedural requirements are for each cemetery.

Considering Cremation

The alternative of cremation has increased in the
United States over the past two decades. The process is
much less expensive than traditional burial. While other
countries like Japan and England choose cremation as the
primary method of disposition, in the United States, approximately 17 percent of all deceased persons are now
cremated. In states like California and Florida, the rate is
higher. In 1990 in California, cremation was chosen in
40.12 percent of total deaths; in Florida it was 34.46 percent. Costs for cremation vary from $500 to $1,000. Generally, non-profit memorial societies can arrange the
cremation process for less.

Many choose cremation because of the expense involved in burial services. Others believe that it symbolizes
the ashes-to-ashes and dust-to dust concept. Cremation is
often chosen in order to dispose of the body immediately.
The families of a person cremated can, and usually do,
hold memorial or funeral services just as families of a
person being buried. Counselors on grieving recommend
that people who choose cremation follow other traditional
customs of funeral or memorial services. Friends and
members of the family may attend a worship service or
ceremony to commemorate the deceased person's life and
death. The service can be in a religious house of worship,
in a person's home, favorite scenic location, or in a funeral
home.

Out of State Disposal

If you wish to be cremated and then shipped out of state
for burial, this too is possible. Shipping fees range from
$50 to $75. The cremains can be shipped by U.S. Post or
UPS to your relative or any person handling the final
disposition, or to an out-of-town funeral director. A

certificate of cremation should accompany the cremains when shipped. The cemetery will need this for their records and to perform the burial. Your local memorial society or funeral director can provide further information.

CREMATION INFORMATION SHEET

Name: _____ Date_____

I wish to be cremated: _____Yes_____No

I wish there to be a visitation and/or service before I am cremated: _____Yes_____No

I would like to have a memorial service after cremation:

_____Yes_____No

If yes, where: _____

I would like my cremains returned in an urn: _____

Type of Urn: _____Price Range: _____

I would like my cremains buried:_____Yes_____No

If yes, where: _____

I would like my cremains scattered:_____Yes_____No

If yes, where:_____

(Please check with your funeral director for legal requirements.)

I do/do not have a pacemaker: _____

I wish my cremains returned to: Name: _____

_____

I prefer direct cremation with no service: _____

I prefer direct cremation with a memorial service following: _

_____

I do/do not want my cremains at the memorial service: _____

I would like to have a picture of me placed in view at my memorial service: _____

It is located at: _____

Description of Picture:_____

_____

Flowers or Memorial Donation: _____

_____

Please remove all jewelry before cremation and return to: __

_____

NOTES

CHAPTER 5

ORGAN DONATION AND BODY BEQUEATHAL

...The only gift is a portion of yourself.

The gift without the giver is bare.

—James Russell Lowell

In the past 20 years, organ transplant operations have greatly advanced. Many people donate their kidneys, eyes, pancreas, liver, hearts, lungs, and other anatomical parts for such purposes. Skin can be donated for burn victims with severe burns, and even certain bones can be transplanted.

Organ Donation

Young to middle-aged people admitted to an emergency room who will eventually die because of their injuries are the best potential donors. If tests show the person to be "brain dead," the organs are kept alive using a respirator. Most organs can be saved for a day or so, but doctors prefer to transplant organs as quickly as possible to avoid tissue damage. When "brain death" occurs, medical personnel need to get permission quickly to remove organs. You can indicate that you wish to donate parts of your body for these purposes on the back of your driver's license in some states, on a Uniform Donor Card, or in your will or Living Will (see the Resource Section).

Organs are in short supply and greatly needed, particularly kidneys, hearts, and livers. Certain factors must be taken into consideration. If a person's heart stops beating and a respirator is not used to preserve organs, only tissues such as skin, bones and corneas can be used. The Uniform Anatomical Gift Act, created in 1968, governs state laws concerning organ donations. Any person over 18 years of age may agree to donate part or all of his body after death.

Doctors and nurses may also request permission from the family of a dying person at the time of death if appropriate. This could cause great stress if the survivors do not know the wishes of the deceased. It is advised that you discuss with your family exactly what your wishes are. Make them known to your physician and put them in writing. Such a decision may easily give the gift of life to another needy individual.

If a person is to donate an organ, his body is put on a respirator which pumps life-saving oxygen into his organs, even though they are "brain dead." An operation is performed within 12 to 48 hours to remove the particular organ sought. The organ is rushed to a recipient's hospital for the transplant. There is seldom communication between the donor family and the recipient for reasons of confidentiality. Donors are not charged anything for the surgical or shipping costs.

Keep in mind that the age of a donor is important. Medical personnel want organs from relatively young people in order for the organ to function for several decades. For instance, heart donors should be under 30 to 35 years of age.

Uniform Donor Cards can be obtained from The Living Bank, Medic Alert and Organ Donors Canada and also from the Continental Association of Funeral and Memorial Societies, and Kidney Foundations (see the Resource Section).

Eye Donations

There are a great number of people whose eyesight can be restored by corneal transplants. For this reason, donation of your eyes is an important service. Eyes must be removed within a few hours of death. This may be done at the hospital or in a funeral home by trained personnel. The individual's body may still be left to a medical school after eye donation, and it makes no difference in the viewing of the body. However, some medical schools will not accept a body after any parts have been removed.

Write or call your nearest Eye Bank to pledge your eyes and carry a Uniform Donor Card. Let your physician and family know in writing of your wishes. Even those who wear glasses may donate since eyes are used for medical research also. Many people benefit when individuals donate their eyes, offering the gift of eyesight to another.

Eyeglasses which will no longer be used may also be donated to New Eyes For The Needy, the local Lions' Club, and other organizations that recycle them. Check the eye bank in your community for information. A listing of eye banks in several major cities is contained in the Resource Section.

Body Donation

Medical and dental schools need thousands of bodies each year for research and teaching purposes. It is possible to store bodies for a limited time before transportation if necessary. Depending on the location of the school, there is a greater need in small, more rural locations. At times an oversupply exists in some major cities. It is wise to have an alternative plan, such as burial or cremation, in case bequeathal of the body does not occur.

If you wish to donate your body to medical research after death, it is very important to check with the institution for which your gift is intended. Determine what the conditions for accepting a body are. Some will refuse bodies that have been autopsied or mutilated by a violent death. Bodies missing major organs or limbs may also be rejected. The age and weight at the time of death is another consideration. Families may request from the designated donor school or organization information about the final disposition of the remains.

Donation Procedures

If there is to be no funeral or viewing requiring the body of the deceased, then it may be transported immediately to the medical school. Some schools will pay this cost, others won't. Most pay the expense within a certain distance within the state. Most funeral homes are willing to work with medical schools. These schools are aware of the psychological benefits of a funeral or memorial service to the family and the loved ones of the deceased.

A funeral home's services will usually be required if the body is to be flown by airplane. Embalming may be required. The funeral home should check with the school as to what type of embalming is acceptable.

Legal Paperwork

The paperwork required to accept the donation of a body after death is uncomplicated. All that is necessary is a death certificate and a transportation permit. The funeral director will coordinate obtaining signatures from the physician in charge at the time of death. The death certificate will be sent to the Board of Health, who in turn, issues a transportation permit upon receipt. The body may then be transported by the necessary means. Bodies may even be delivered by private transportation if desired.

Anyone who wants to donate part or all of his body after death should not hesitate to do so. But make your wishes known to your loved ones and to a hospital. Such donations are beneficial to the living and the donors can feel that they have left a precious gift. Many people take comfort in knowing that they have offered sight or life to another even when their own has ended.

ORGAN DONATION FORM

Name _____

After death I prefer to donate these organs:

_____

To: _____

_____

Autopsy (If family or doctor requests): _____

After death I prefer to donate my body to: _____

_____

Date of Arrangements: _____

_____

Location of paperwork: _____

_____

Contact:_____

_____

Signed _____

Date _____

NOTES

CHAPTER 6

LEGAL AND FINANCIAL ASPECTS

...Death is the goal of all life
— Sigmund Freud

When a person inquires about funeral arrangements, the funeral home will provide the costs of each individual funeral item and service in person or by telephone. A list of costs will be given if requested in person. The list discloses legal rights and requirements regarding funeral arrangements. It must include information on embalming, cash advance sales, (such as newspaper notices or flowers), caskets for cremation, and required purchases.

You have the right to choose only the goods and services you want. The funeral home must provide this right in writing as well as disclose any specific law that requires you to purchase a particular item. For example, most cemeteries require a vault or less expensive liner for burial.

THE FEDERAL TRADE COMMISSION (FTC)

In April of 1984, the Federal Trade Commission (FTC) developed a trade regulation rule concerning funeral industry practices called the Funeral Rule. Its purpose is to enable consumers to obtain information about funeral arrangements and make it easier for a person to select only those goods and services they want or need and to pay for only those they select. For example, you can research the cost of individual items over the telephone. The funeral home must provide a written price list of the goods and services available when asked in person to do so.

The general price list discloses important legal rights and requirements regarding funeral arrangements. It must include information on embalming, cash advance sales (such as newspaper notices or flowers), caskets for cremation, and required purchases.

Under the Funeral Rule, funeral providers are prohibited from telling you a particular funeral item or service can indefinitely preserve the body of the deceased in the grave or that certain caskets or vaults will keep out water, dirt, and other gravesite substances.

All states have a licensing board that is responsible for regulation of the funeral industry. You may contact the licensing board in your state for information or help. The Conference of Funeral Service Examining Boards, 520 E. Van Trees St. PO Box 497, Washington, Indiana 47501 represents the licensing boards of 47 states and will provide information on the various state laws and respond to consumer inquiries or complaints. The National Funeral Directors Association can also provide information on funeral practices. Lists of Funeral Associations and memorial societies are provided in the Resource Section.

PREPAID PLANS

Pre-need arrangements account for as much as 75 percent of all funeral home sales today. Many families choose to select and pre-pay for vaults, caskets, cemetery plots, burial and cremation services, and other ceremonies to alleviate the anguish of making those decisions later.

There are several ways to pre-fund funeral expenses if you wish to do so. Pre-funding offers you the advantage of paying for your funeral when you can afford it. It helps to prevent possible financial and emotional burdens to your loved ones. If you decide to pre-fund, select a funeral home you trust, ask what options are available and determine whether you have a funeral contract (guaranteed) or final expense funding (no guarantee).

Most states have legislation related to prepaid funerals, requirements for how monies can be set aside, conditions for cancellation, and regulations concerning who can sell prepaid funerals. Any state funeral board, attorney general's office, or insurance commission can guide you with your inquiries about state requirements. In a pre-paid plan the cost of the cemetery plot, casket, service, burial, or cremation process can be paid in advance to save money and to remove a burden from survivors. There are many optional prepayment plans.

When deciding to purchase a prepaid plan, look for one that has a revocable, guaranteed price that will guarantee the funeral you desire regardless of future price increases, and will allow for a partial or full refund if you change your plans. Unfortunately, these are not available in every state. Be sure you understand the details of paying in one lump sum or in installments.

Insurance

A second way to pre-fund your funeral costs is by purchasing a special insurance policy that provides benefits for funeral expenses. Be cautious. Some policies have an established date you must live beyond or the policy only pays a part of your final expenses. There are several questions you should ask if you choose this option:

- What happens if the funeral home goes out of business?

- What happens if you relocate to another area, another state?
- Is the prepayment refundable in part or in full?
- Does the prepayment cover cost increases?
- Who gets the account interest and who pays the taxes on that interest?

If you select an insurance policy, be certain that payments keep up with inflation and guarantee coverage for the funeral plan you have chosen. Also, check on cancellation and what cash value you would receive if you change your mind.

PRE-FUNDING ALTERNATIVES

Trust Fund

A Trust Fund Agreement is one in which you deposit a specified amount of money in either one lump sum or installments. This fund is managed by a trustee (yourself, a bank, or a professional funeral organization) and is used to pay for specific funeral services and merchandise. There are two basic methods of agreement concerning trusts. You can let the funeral organization take the risk, i.e., that the interest earned will keep up with inflation or you can contract up front with the funeral home to guarantee that no matter how long you live, the merchandise you have selected and paid for will not increase in price. You can also put the money in trust in your own name and gamble on the interest keeping up with inflation to cover costs in the future. Formal trust agreements are regulated by most states and audited for proper record keeping.

Totten Trust

In addition to establishing a trust or purchasing an insurance policy, you may also choose to establish your own specific bank account, buy additional life insurance, or make special investments with the plan to use the proceeds for your funeral expenses. Check with your local bank or credit union about establishing a savings account listing a beneficiary or a "Totten Trust." This is also called a "Revocable Living Trust" in which you earn the interest and are able to change your mind about the use of the money. When you die, the funds go to the designated beneficiary, either a family member, friend, or a funeral home who has been instructed to use these monies for your funeral.

The American Association of Retired Persons (AARP) encourages people to pre-arrange their plans and budget for their funeral. Concerning pre-paying, the organization believes the best way is to have an account that is under your own control.

Paying in advance can give you the satisfaction of knowing that you have helped relatives or loved ones with an unpleasant task. It is an act of kindness and love to your family and friends. Investigate wisely and after understanding the alternatives, make your choice.

By knowing what you want, understanding the prices of goods, services, and options, an appropriate funeral or memorial service can be obtained at a reasonable price.

Understanding Price Lists

The "General Price List" from a funeral home is a list of prices for goods and/or services provided, either for pre-need arrangements (pre-planned) or for at need arrangements. The Federal Trade Commission FTC requires that funeral homes break down prices into an itemized list for services:

1) **Professional Services** - Includes such items as services of the staff, coordinating service plans, cemetery arrangements, crematory, and transportation.

2) **Additional Services** - includes direction of the funeral, supervision and attendants for visitation,

arrangement of flowers and supervision for services at the graveside. Embalming falls under this section which includes preparation of the body, cosmetology, and hairdressing. Hairdressing for a woman may not be included. A licensed funeral director can normally fix a man's hair with ease, but special care of a hairdresser may be required for a female which could cost an additional $35.00 to $70.00, depending on the area and what needs to be done.

3) **Transportation Services** - "Transportation" includes transfer of remains from the place of death to the funeral home. This takes into account the distance travelled to pick up a body and return it to the funeral home, use of a vehicle, and use of an administrative vehicle for necessary paperwork and legal requirements. Other automotive costs may be listed for use of a car to lead the procession to the place of burial and the use of a car for the family. Some funeral homes use limousines for this service.

4) **Other** - The section called, "Other," includes thank you cards, register books and memorial folders or cards. Remember the above sections list costs for services only. Flowers, cemetery charges, escort services, organist or soloist, and other outside charges are not included. Flowers can be provided through the funeral home or ordered separately by the family. Chapel rental, gratuity fees, and an honorarium to the clergyperson performing the service are other items to be paid. These are all separate and should be considered cash advance items. Many funeral homes will pay for the cash advance items for you so you

only have one bill if you desire. Other funeral homes may want you to pay for those items in advance, but you will find that most will pay for them and then bill you. In making pre-arrangements, these items cannot usually be paid for in advance, with the exception of cemetery charges.

Most funeral homes offer a "package" price on service items. You will find this generally to be less expensive than paying item by item. You will need to compare what you want to include with the package price to determine which is less expensive. If you want a normal service with viewing, or if you select cremation, there will be another price list for this service. Also, if the remains are to be shipped elsewhere, there will be a separate charge for this service. An example of the charges for services of a funeral home follows. It is from a California funeral home and will give you an idea of what to expect.

Example Of A Funeral Home's General Price List (1992)

Minimum Services $695.00

(Includes arrangement of the funeral, consultation with the family and clergy, filing of necessary notices, and authorizations by the funeral director and staff.) Fee included in charges for direct cremations, immediate burials and forwarding or receiving of remains.

Additional Services $125.00

(Includes, but is not limited to, the coordination of funeral or memorial service, supervision and attendants for services at Chapel, Graveside or Cryptside.)

Weekends, Holidays or After Hours - Service Charge ..$100.00

Embalming $125.00

Embalming is not required by law except in certain cases. It may be necessary for body preservation if a service with viewing is desired.

Alternate Care $100.00

If embalming is declined and final disposition of the deceased is not completed within 24 hours from the time of death, refrigeration is requested.

Other Preparation of the Deceased $75.00

(Includes preparation & casketing of the deceased other than embalming)

Facilities $100.00

Use of facilities for viewing or visitation or for funeral ceremony or for set up procedure at church or other outside facility.

Transportation (within 50 Miles)

Funeral Coach (hearse) $150.00

Service Vehicle (e.g., flower van) $110.00

Limousine (minimum 3 hours) $175.00

Utility Vehicle (e.g., To arrange State/local documents)

....$100.00

Other Merchandise

Acknowledgement Cards (50 pkg.) and Register Book .$15.00 to $65.00

Memorial Cards or Folders (per 100) ....$ 35.00 to $50.00

Caskets are priced from ....$395.00 to $18,000.00

Other Burial Containers from ....$380.00 to $9,143.00

(A complete burial price list will be provided)

Cremation Options From ....$669.00 to $1690.00

(Includes transportation of the deceased to our facility within 50 miles and minimum services of funeral director and staff) For a direct cremation an unfinished wood box or other alternative container (cardboard, pressed wood etc.) may be used.

Direct cremation with container provided by family......$669.00

Direct cremation with alternative container $806.00

Cremation with a request date by the family, delivery or disposition $739.00

Cremation with graveside services $839.00

Cremation with memorial Service $995.00

(Includes attendant and use of chapel)

Cremation with deceased present for viewing. $1095.00

(Includes embalming, other preparation, visitation, chapel service, facilities, personnel, music)

Placement of cremated remains (by Aircraft)

At Sea $130.00

Delivery of cremains within 50 Mile............................$50.00

Shipment via Registered Mail (Within U.S.) $50.00

Shipment via scheduled airline (plus airfare) $75.00

Immediate Burials $695.00

(Includes transportation of the deceased to our facility, minimum services of funeral director and staff, and essential facilities and transportation charges)

Minimum Care Services

Forwarding to another Funeral Home $754.00

Receiving from another Funeral Home $729.00

Example of Funeral Service Costs - Packages

Package options can generally be purchased at less cost than choosing items separately.

1. Total Service $1594.00

This option includes services of Funeral Director, administrative, and professional staff for coordination and direction of funeral service, preparation of the death certificate, other necessary state and local documents, transfer of deceased from place of death to mortuary, embalming/alternative care of remains, use of facilities for viewing, funeral service, or for set up procedures at church or outside facility, funeral coach, service vehicle and utility vehicle. (If above items were purchased separately, the cost would be $1705.00)

2. Standard Service $1494.00

This option includes services of Funeral Director, administrative staff, and professional staff for coordination of funeral service, preparation of death certificate and other necessary state and legal documents, transfer of deceased from place of death to mortuary, embalming/alternate care of remains, use of facilities for viewing, funeral service or set up procedures at church or outside facility, funeral coach and utility vehicle. (If purchased separately, the cost would be $1595.00)

3. Basic Service $1394.00

This option includes services of Funeral Director, administrative staff, and professional staff for coordination and direction of graveside service, preparation of death certificate and other necessary state and legal documents, transfer of deceased from place of death to mortuary, embalming/alternative care of remains, use of facilities for viewing, funeral coach and utility vehicle. (If purchased separately, the cost would be $1495.00)

Casket and burial vault price lists should include all casket and vaults the funeral home has to offer. They will usually start at the least expensive and work up to the higher priced merchandise and include a description of the items. The burial vault price list will be the same, however, most vault companies have a handling fee to add to the vault price. This may include set-up and lowering devices, tent and chairs for graveside services and maybe even a sealing fee. You can determine roughly what the funeral will cost by adding the Service Charges, Cash Advance Items, Casket and Vault prices, and other special fees.

Since a funeral is a major expense for most families, discuss all prices in detail with your local funeral director and cemetery.

SOCIAL SECURITY BENEFITS

The Social Security Administration offers a lump sum benefit of $255.00 toward burial expenses of eligible people, i.e., to the surviving spouse or dependent minor. You must apply to your local office for this benefit. They will also assist in adjusting the monthly social security benefit after the death of a spouse and explain how to return a monthly benefit check that was received since death occurred if applicable. For information you can call your local social security office or the Social Security Administration at (800) 772-1213, their toll free number.

Supplemental Security Income (SSI)

If planning ahead, you can set aside a certain dollar amount, usually up to approximately $1500.00 for burial and an average of $3000.00 for a casket and vault which will not be counted as a resource if you are concerned about eligibility for Supplemental Security Income (SSI). The requirements vary from state to state. The money must be specifically set aside for burial and must be separately identifiable from other resources. If you use any of the burial funds for other purposes, your future SSI payments will be reduced by that amount. Contact your local Social Security Office for more information.

Special Services/benefits

Special services may be available and can be coordinated through the funeral director. For example, members of certain groups like the Veterans of Foreign Wars (VFW) or American Legion may provide on request special graveside services. In one type of service at the graveside, the folding and presentation of the American Flag takes place after readings by leaders of the post, or an honor guard may give a rifle salute. Most VFW and American Legion posts will provide these services for deceased members of their organizations.

Other groups, including some women's auxiliary groups, provide special rituals for certain organizations as a way to honor fallen members. Some of these include the Daughters of the American Revolution, Sons of the American Revolution, Order of the Eastern Star, Masonic Lodges, and Loyal Order of Moose. Your funeral director will contact the appropriate organization upon your request. Include your wishes in your pre-arrangement plans so your family will know of them. List the dates you joined a particular group, your position within it or any special duties or committees you or your loved one served on. This will assist the funeral director in making your final wishes complete.

Veterans Benefits

Benefits available to veterans, their spouses and minor children include free burial in a national cemetery for those meeting requirements. These benefits include a grave marker, flag, and perpetual care. According to a January 1991 publication, *Federal Benefits For Veterans and Dependents,* published by the Department of Veterans Affairs, veterans discharged or separated from active duty, under conditions other than dishonorable, who have completed the required period of service, and U.S. Armed Forces members who die on active duty, are eligible for burial in one of the VA's 113 national cemeteries. Spouses and dependent children of eligible living and deceased veterans or armed forces members are also eligible. Gravesites in national cemeteries cannot be reserved. Funeral directors or others making burial arrangements must apply at the time of death. The National Cemetery System does not conduct burials on weekends when most offices are closed. A weekend caller will be directed to one of three strategically located offices which remain open to schedule burials during the coming week.

The VA provides headstones and markers for the graves of vets anywhere in the world. Flat bronze, granite or marble and upright marble types are available. Bronze niche markers are also available. Headstones are inscribed with the name, year of birth and death, and branch of service. Optional items that may be inscribed at VA expense are military grade, war service, months and days of the dates of birth and death, an emblem reflective of one's beliefs (such as a Christian Cross), valor awards received, and the Purple Heart. Additional items may be inscribed at private expense.

When burial is at a national cemetery, the headstone is ordered by the national cemetery staff who will place it on the grave. When burial occurs in a cemetery other than a national cemetery or a state veterans' cemetery, the headstone must be applied for separately. It will be shipped at government expense to the consignee designated on the application. To date nine states have no cemetery providing free burial for military veterans and their families.

Unfortunately, many of the national cemeteries are reaching capacity. Also VA burial rules and policies change periodically, so contact a local VA office for current information.

The VA will also provide memorial headstones or markers to memorialize an eligible veteran whose remains are not available for burial. The memorial marker may be provided for placement in a plot at other than a national cemetery. In such a case, however, the VA does not pay the cost of the plot or the placement of the marker. It will pay the shipping costs to the consignee designated on the application. For additional details, contact the Department of Veteran Affairs, Washington, DC 20420. Forms and assistance are available at VA regional offices.

Public Aid Funerals

Certain states provide public aid funerals for those without means. For a modest amount, the decedent will be provided a casket, grave liner, and a graveside service. The cemetery will be reimbursed by the state for one burial site, and for the opening and closing of the grave according to the state law. Unfortunately the amount set aside in many states is not adequate and does not cover the costs incurred by the funeral home and the cemetery. There will usually be no visitation or funeral services in such a situation, only preparation and graveside service for the deceased. If you should become financially indigent because of a catastrophic illness or other misfortune, your prepaid funeral arrangement is protected by law if it was set up properly. Your funeral director or memorial society can inform you of the requirements and laws in your state.

Funeral Check List And Expense Sheet

Costs

Death Certificates _____   Number of copies_____

Obituary Notice_____

Method of Disposal

    Burial .... _____

    Cremation .... _____

Embalming .... _____

Cemetery Plot... _____

Outer Container

    Concrete... _____

    Steel .... _____

Installation of markers on grave .... _____

Casket.. _____

Funeral service .... _____

Visitation... _____

Guest Book.. _____

Flowers .... _____

Hearse .... _____

Limousines.. _____

Other .... _____

TOTAL COSTS.. _____

Income

Veteran .... _____

Social Security .... _____

Private Fund, Insurance, etc... _____

Other .... _____

TOTAL INCOME.. _____

NET COSTS... _____

NOTES

CHAPTER 7

OLD AND NEW FUNERAL RITUALS

> . . .Death is the sole equality on Earth
> — Phillip J. Bailey

Ancient Death Rituals and Burial Customs

Funeral and burial customs have long been a ritual passage for humans. They date back beyond the Egyptians who spent much of life preparing for death and the needs of the spirit. The ancient kings of Egypt, or Pharaohs, built the great pyramids as tombs. Bodies were elaborately embalmed for preservation and treated with herbs, spices, and chemicals to turn the corpse into a mummy.

The mummy of a king was wrapped in several layers of cotton and placed in a carved wooden case (sarcophagus) which was sealed into a vault of stone. Jewels and gold were buried with the mummy. Everything needed for the journey to another life was put in the tomb; tools, food, chariots, thrones, and even slaves and wives.

From earliest times, humankind has practiced a variety of ceremonies designed to bury the dead and help the surviving loved ones. Because humans are gregarious and their interaction is a part of the definition of the very meaning of life, such ceremonies are important to the healing process when death occurs.

Burial customs differ widely in different geographic locations amongst different peoples. A look at some of them reveals the different beliefs about life and death people have had. You may want your burial plans to reflect your own or your loved one's beliefs just as the ceremony for Veronica in Chapter 1 reflected her personality, her religion, and her essence.

In New Zealand, the Maoris placed a dying person in a special hut, dressed in his best finery. After an elaborate ceremony, the body was washed and placed in public view where mourners, wearing wreaths of green leaves wailed and slashed their own bodies with knives. Chants of praise were sung. The body was then wrapped in a mat and placed on a high platform or in a hollow tree. A lavish feast followed in which the mourners gave gifts to the dead person's family. The bones of the deceased were cleaned at a later time, colored with red earth and finally placed in a sacred cave. The ceremonial hut was burned.

In South Asia and India, cremation is practiced. The body is carried to a special area, usually near a sacred temple, and burned on a pile of logs. The ashes are thrown into the sacred river, the Ganges. Many Hindus desire to be cremated by the banks of the river and have their ashes thrown into the holy water.

In the Southwest United States, the Navaho Indians were fearful of death and of the spirits of the dead. Once a person died, his house was burned. Relatives prepared the body and buried it, then returned home by a different route so the dead one's spirit could not follow. The mourners then stood in an open smoke fire to purify themselves.

Europe

Burial practices differ considerably in Europe. In some countries, like Great Britain, privately owned but government regulated funeral homes handle the disposal of the dead as in the United States. Some religions insist on burial of the dead while others recommend cremation. Cremation is encouraged by many authorities to save money for families, and to reduce the encroachment of cemeteries on scarce farming land.

In several other European countries, the State is responsible for the burial or cremation of the dead. A basic burial or cremation service is provided as a service of the State. Families must pay extra for any equipment or service above that normally provided. In some eastern European countries, where agricultural land is at a premium, the State provides a burial plot at no charge for 20 years. At the end of that period, the remains of the deceased are removed, put in an urn, and the cemetery plot used for another body. For an additional fee the surviving family can pay to have the body remain in the plot for another 20 years.

United States

In the United States today, funeral services range from traditional or religious services, to cremation, bequeathal of the body to a medical organization, or private family burials. Some individuals prefer no service at all. On the West Coast, a large percentage of the dead are cremated, but in the Midwest the vast majority of people are buried. In New Orleans, because of the high water table of the ground, people are buried above ground in crypts or vaults.

Following is a discussion of the various methods currently practiced to help you in making your own decision.

TRADITIONAL BURIAL CUSTOMS

Traditional burial in the ground is at present the preference of most Americans, but the option of cremation or incineration of the body is increasing in use. In traditional burials the individual selects a vault and casket, purchases a cemetery plot, and plans a service according to his last wishes.

Most formal religions include ritualized ceremonies to commemorate the dead, but today there is a trend to individualize these rituals and make them more meaningful to those directly involved. Because every situation is different, there are many needs to be met by a death service. Some of the more common ones have to do with human relationships.

There is a need to help the loved ones work through their grief when a death occurs in a family or circle of friends. A need to identify the deceased's place in this life, a need for relief of guilt, and a need to affirm the values that an individual stood for in life are common. Often there is a need to re-establish the relationship of the survivors. For example, when a parent dies, the relationship of a surviving child changes forever.

There is also a common need to remember with joy the life of an elderly person. If he had failed in health prior to death, it is helpful to remember the prime of his life and what that symbolized.

The most basic common need is the need for emotional support. The ceremony is performed to help the survivors accept and mourn the death of their loved one. Readings and eulogies often are addressed in a way that touches on the values of the closest survivors. Religious people often want to be remembered in a formal ceremony based on their beliefs. Others who are not formally religious may want a combination of a traditional ceremony and some particular individual services. Many young people who die from tragic illnesses like AIDS wish to prepare their own ceremony in order to be remembered according to their own wishes. All societies practice a variety of different ceremonies to remember their dead. Each individual has the right to plan for and even write himself, a service for his own death.

RELIGIOUS RITUALS and SERVICES

Protestant

In the United States, the majority of funeral services are based on religious beliefs and customs. Protestant services, which can vary in custom from area to area and denomination to denomination are widely requested. Often a Protestant pastor will write a special, individualized service to use along with particular readings or scriptures from the Bible or other book. These funerals are generally preceded by a visitation period with an open of closed casket, depending on the deceased and the family's wishes. Flowers to a diminishing degree or other gifts are sent to express sadness and concern to the family members or a particular charity organization is designated to receive donations. Many churches accept donations in memory of the deceased also.

Protestant services include lessons from the scripture that relate to the Christian concept of resurrection. Prayers, singing of hymns, a sermon, and group readings are common. These services are often held in a facility provided for a fee, by the mortuary instead of in the deceased's church.

Catholic

Relatively formal guidelines for funerals are followed by the Roman Catholic Church. However, in today's world, some priests will design a special service which incorporates the traditions of the Church with modern readings, songs, or sermons. A Rosary or prayer service is held prior to the funeral and sometimes a wake (with open casket if desired) is held at the funeral home on the evening before the funeral. Flowers or gifts are sent to the family. Often, a family will request that donations to a certain charity be made. Many choose to make a donation to the church in memory of the deceased. Friends and families request that a mass be said for the repose of the soul of the deceased.

From the funeral home, the casket (now closed) is taken to the Church where a funeral Mass is said for the deceased. The group then proceeds to the gravesite where additional liturgical ceremonies are performed. Once forbidden by Church law, Catholics may now choose cremation as an alternative to burial in the ground.

Jewish

Jewish services vary between the Orthodox, the Conservative, and the Reformed branches. Usually the funeral itself is considered the beginning of ceremonies instead of the end. Shorter than most of the Christian rituals, the Jewish ceremony consists of affirming that a life was lived, and prayers that praise life. Jewish families often prefer that contributions to specific charities be made rather than the sending of flowers.

In traditional Jewish families, the survivors remain at home for seven days after the funeral and friends and relatives visit and offer support. The emphasis is on people sharing feelings and memories rather than on religious teachings.

Some may attend services every day for a full year to remember the deceased. Often the memorial stone or tablet of the deceased is not unveiled until months after the funeral. This gives family and friends another opportunity to gather together. On the anniversary of death, the deceased's name is read aloud during synagogue service.

Humanist Ceremonies

Not all people are formally religious, and some may request a funeral or a memorial service from a church with which they had a past relationship. Others desire no funeral at all. Many families and friends will gather together to acknowledge the death of the loved one, share grief, and offer support. A friend or family member may lead the service or sometimes a pastor is asked to conduct the ceremony, avoiding religious imagery. Readings of poetry, singing and readings of literature may be included. Usually, the philosophy of the deceased is emphasized. Group participation is encouraged and often offers support to the survivors as well as the other mourners.

There are many different ways to hold a funeral service. If you should desire a humanist rather than a traditional service, a memorial society or the funeral director of your choice can advise you. Many people choose to write their own ceremony or have a family member do so. Just as in traditional religious funerals, such services are beneficial to the survivors and help the grieving process.

EXAMPLES OF CONTEMPORARY FUNERAL SERVICES

Traditional Service with Burial

TOM, a loved and respected businessman, died at the age of 60 from cancer. Over the years he had helped many people in business and participated in the congregation of Reverend Robert Schuller at the Crystal Cathedral in Orange County, California. Over three hundred people from the church, community and business associations attended the service.

Tom's children and the pastor prepared a warm and meaningful memorial ceremony in his memory. The adult children and their families, including several young grandchildren ranging in age from 2 to 9, attended. An organist played Tom's favorite hymns, including "Amazing Grace."

Reverend Schuller, a close personal friend, delivered the eulogy, remembering Tom for all the good he had brought to his church and community. The organ, piano and other string instruments resounded throughout the glass cathedral. The family had prepared a series of color slides commemorating Tom's life, from his love of horses to his many travels. Appropriate music for each life passage accompanied the slide presentation. The pictures spanned his infancy, boyhood, his military service, his first marriage (he lost his first wife at a young age to cancer) the birth of his children, his second marriage and the birth of his grandchildren. One showed him holding his three year old daughter who died from leukemia. It was a moving life collage.

Readings were given from scripture and special poets. At one point, a moment of quiet contemplation in memory of Tom was called for. During the playing of soft music, the front wall of the church, made entirely of glass, opened slowly, allowing bright sunshine to pour down on an uprising fountain of water. It was a breathtaking ceremony held in beautiful surroundings and a fitting memorial to one who had contributed much to his community and church in life.

After the service, family and friends gathered for a buffet meal in the church meeting room to remember Tom, buoyed by the befitting and appropriate memorial his children and friends had arranged for him.

Memorial Service

DOROTHY, after a long illness in which she suffered great depression, was diagnosed with cancer. When she finally found out she had a short time to live, her depression lifted, she made her peace with God, and said she was ready to go. At first, she said she didn't want a service at all, but her many friends told her that they would have one anyway so she might as well accept it. Dorothy was a very accomplished musician and had accompanied several local artists. She was also the organist for her church. At this point, she became enthusiastic about planning her own service, calling friends and asking them to perform and sing. After her death, the memorial service was held at her church with her son giving the eulogy describing his remembrances of her. Then he and two other members of his musical trio performed his parent's favorite song, "My Blue Heaven." One woman sang "The Lord's Prayer," another sang "When You Walk Through A Storm" from *Carousel* and the final and most moving tribute was from her dearest friend who sang "My Buddy," turning to look at Dorothy's picture which was displayed at the front of the church.

Cremation

SCOTT, a 25 year old young man, contracted the AIDS virus in 1983. This was only a year or so after it had been identified, and he had struggled before receiving a diagnosis. Always a practical and intelligent person, he set about to deal with his illness and impending death in a businesslike manner. When his mother shared this information with a close friend, she said he discussed the matter of death arrangements with a minister, a woman who was a long-time friend, rather than with his parents. He wanted to spare his mother and father the pain. Scott wrote down what he wanted, a simple memorial service with only his parents, sister, and close friends attending.

He chose cremation and wanted his ashes to be spread over the Presidio, an area of park-like beauty near San Francisco. Scott chose one particular religious song for his service, "Jesus Loves Me." He had experienced discrimination as a member of the gay community and felt this traditional song that most Christians learn in childhood to be reassuring. He was a brilliant and handsome young man, a musical genius, who had managed to complete one year of college in his senior year in high school. He suffered, struggling to maintain life, and his death was an untimely one. His parents respected his last wishes and the memorial service was held in a nearby church. The minister read from Scott's favorite scriptures, spoke warmly about his friendship with her and others, and remembered the many successes in Scott's young life. Haunting flute music, Scott's favorite instrument, played in the background. The song, "Jesus Loves Me" was played. It was a tribute to Scott himself that he had the courage to ask for exactly what he wanted. After the memorial service, his parents and sister made a trip to the Presidio area in San Francisco and spread his ashes on a grassy hill overlooking the ocean.

In the past decade, AIDS has caused many untimely deaths. Scott's mother, who started a support group for Mothers of AIDS patients after his death, has since attended many funeral services.

She points out that many people who have died from AIDS expressed their desire to take charge, to control the last act of their lives. The majority of AIDS patients choose cremation, rather than burial in the ground. The services requested range from traditional to contemporary. There is great emphasis on the celebration of life at the funeral service. Most persons who have died of AIDS plan personal touches. They want family and close friends in attendance. The services are upbeat and positive, with shared testimonials from friends. The 'Passing of the Peace' where people shake hands and say "Peace Be With You" is a familiar ritual. Some have even planned the menu for a meal to be shared by friends after the service. In lieu of flowers, many request the release of multi-colored balloons into the air, with a single white balloon, symbolizing the life of the deceased, being released at the end by a parent or loved one.

LANG, after undergoing the first open heart surgery, did not survive a second surgery two months later. His death was not a total shock, but it was unexpected by his family who asked themselves "What do we do now?"

His wife, Norma, and children were of the Catholic faith but Lang was not. Because Lang had been a sailor in World War II and had expressed his wishes to have his ashes scattered at sea, his family made arrangements for cremation and a memorial service. The night before the service, his son and two daughters met to recall their special fond memories of their father. They put together a huge collage of snapshots to be displayed at the funeral home.

At the service, the Priest spoke mainly about Lang and Norma's long and loving marriage and asked for a moment of silence to recall favorite memories of Lang. His son-in-law gave the eulogy. It was comprised of memories of Lang by his children, the type of man he was and included many of his favorite expressions which were delivered humorously in Lang's own manner of speaking. Norma chose two modern songs that symbolized their relationship; "The Wind Beneath My Wings" as sung by Bette Midler and "Unforgettable" as sung by Natalie and Nat King Cole. Everyone was invited back to the family home for a buffet provided by neighbors and friends.

That night, close family members fashioned wreathes from flowers that had been sent and the next morning, relatives went to the harbor to board the boat specially rented for the occasion. They were taken several miles off-shore where Lang's ashes, the flower wreaths, and farewell letters written by his daughters were tossed overboard. As a final gesture, his son and son-in-law took a deck of cards (Lang had been an avid card player) and scattered them over the water. They yelled out Lang's favorite card playing expression, "What do they make Martinis out of?" ("Gin, of course"). Just as the sun broke through the clouds, the boat slowly circled the flowers floating on the water and then returned to shore.

Suicide

When DON, a middle aged school board official who was prominent in the community, committed suicide, his family asked a Unitarian minister to perform the service. It was a sensitive issue because after the suicide many of his friends and family members experienced guilt and felt that they should have done something to prevent the death. With this in mind, the minister conducted the service in the round, which is a service designed to let people speak out. This is similar to a Quaker service where individuals gather and remember the deceased. There were four scheduled speakers and out of the 300 people that attended, more than 15 stood and talked about their friend Don, stressing what he had done for them and how he had helped others. Several close friends shared their memories of Don. This approach addressed the guilt of the family. It let them know that in spite of his suicide, Don's friends still cared and thought highly of him. The service provided great solace to those in attendance.

Services for Infants

CHRISTINA - The death of their three-week old infant, Christina, was particularly hard on her parents. They had been married for twelve years before this first child was conceived. Her arrival was eagerly anticipated. Unfortunately, Christina was born with a defective heart. Several holes were detected and when doctors operated to make repairs, the infant was not strong enough to withstand the surgery. Helen, her mother, had waited many years for this child and wanted to remember her in a special ceremony.

A memorial service was held in which close family and friends participated. Celebrating their Hawaiian heritage, many brought flower leis and wore wreaths of flowers in their hair. Christina was laid out for visitation in a small white bassinet, dressed in a white christening gown. In the short service, the minister baptized the infant, officially naming her Christina, and performed the memorial ceremony. Soft organ music played traditional Hawaiian songs. Prayers and a child's poem, "The Little Tin Soldier" were read. The minister explained that in Hawaii the first birthday of a child is celebrated as the beginning of her life. He announced that the family would have a special memorial for infant Christina on the year anniversary of her birth with a traditional Hawaiian luau celebration.

CONSTANCE - Infant Constance was born with a defect that could not be corrected. The doctor informed the family that her life would be short and encouraged them to spend as much time as possible with her. She died after a short time and the funeral was held a few days later. It was very hard for everyone involved to handle the loss of the newborn. After the service, the funeral director approached the husband with an envelope: inside was a lock of the baby's hair to keep. The father waited until he was home to share with his wife what the funeral director had given him. She was overjoyed that she now had a memento of the little girl she loved so much.

Death of a Teenager

KAREN was seventeen years old when she dropped out of high school. This upset her parents to a great extent. Tragically, they blamed her peers from the local high school for influencing her decision. Later, when she was killed in an automobile accident, the parents held a traditional funeral for close family only and stated that they did not want her friends from the high school to attend. This was extremely upsetting to some of the girls and boys who knew Karen. They approached the school counselor and expressed their sadness, saying they felt as though they were being prevented from mourning the loss of their friend. Weeks later and still upset, one young girl organized a group of friends. Together, they visited Karen's grave, bringing flowers and reading poetry Karen had valued. It helped them to accept her untimely death.

TRENDS IN MEMORIAL AND FUNERAL SERVICES

A common misconception in funeral practice is that the ceremony must conform to traditional ways. If you wish a service that is different from the norm, feel free to innovate. Find a home that will honor your requests. There is a saying that "funerals are for the living." This is true, but you are entitled to have your last wishes respected. Choose what you want. Make your wishes known to your memorial society or funeral director. It is your service. It was your life. It is your responsibility to family and friends.

An emerging trend in funeral service today is the attention given to grief recovery. Some funeral homes now have grief recovery rooms which include libraries and comfortable settings for families to gather, to talk or read. Some homes employ professional grief counselors to assist survivors. They also coordinate special programs such as those for widows, widowers, parents who have lost infants, or survivors of a family in which a member died of a suicide. Other programs are concerned with sadness and depression during the holidays. Many different plans are available. Ask your funeral director about them. They can be very helpful in the grieving process. Following are a few examples of special requests made to funeral homes.

Examples of Special Requests to Funeral Homes

PHILLIP (A Children's Funeral Service) - Ross and Brandon were only two years old when their father, Phillip, was diagnosed with cancer. When he died in 1989 they were three years old. Their mother, Beverly, had discussed having a children's service for the two young boys prior to Phillip's death and he agreed, thinking it a good idea to help them understand his passing. After Phillip died, Beverly asked their pastor and funeral director about a special service for the children. They were startled but agreed to do it. Beverly invited friends and family telling them the service was for the boys and that they were welcome to bring their children if they wanted. Over 25 children, ages three through seven showed up at the funeral home. Phillip had been a free-lance writer, working out of his home and had made friends with several of the neighborhood children.

The service was held at the funeral home the day before the church service, and one hour before the viewing for adults. Beverly began by thanking the children for coming and acknowledging that Ross and Brandon's Daddy had died. She explained that they would go into the next room where his body was lying in a box called a casket. She added that Phillip would look like he was sleeping, but in order to avoid young childrens' fear of going to sleep after they see death, she explained that being dead was different from sleeping. The children were told they could look and touch if they wanted, but warned that Phillip would feel stiff like the arms of a chair. Pastor Pete would talk to them about the death and it was OK to cry and to ask any questions they wanted to.

Two folding chairs had been placed in front of the casket by the funeral director for the children. Every child present climbed up and touched Phillip's body. The pastor, parents and children then sat in a circle on the floor and Pastor Pete told a story about a caterpillar, cocoon, and butterfly. He explained that the soul leaving the body is like the butterfly, the most beautiful part, leaving the cocoon. He then asked for questions and the children asked many, those which adults want to ask but are afraid to. "So where is this heaven anyway?" "Can Phil see us from heaven?" "Can we talk to him?" "Why did Phil die?" "How did he get cancer?" "Where did Phil die and then how did his body get here to the funeral home?" "Why do we have to bury the body?" "Can Phil walk and drive a car in heaven?" "Does God cook for Phil?" "Is Phil happy now?" All the answers, given by Beverly, the parents, and the pastor were open and honest. To some questions, the answer was simply, "We don't know."

The reactions of the children varied with their ages. Most of the three year olds fidgeted, the four year olds stared in interest and asked a few questions; the five year olds asked more questions and the six and seven year olds asked a lot of good questions and many cried. Most of the parents sobbed. The service lasted half an hour and ended with all singing "Jesus Loves Me." The children were then shown a basket of flowers and told they could take one to put in Phil's casket if they wanted as they said goodbye. Most of them did.

The parents who attended were pleased and felt it helped the children, saying that they asked many more questions about Phillip's death at home. Ross and Brandon continued to ask Beverly questions, remembering their friends who cried and Pastor Pete. Beverly's hope is that they will remember their father and the presence of friends so in the future they will continue to ask questions as they mature in order to deepen their understanding and acceptance of the traumatic event.

The above was summarized from an article written by Beverly Godwin for the Spring 1991 edition of Thanatos.

MICHAEL had played the saxophone since he was nine years old. His wife knew of his love for the instrument and Jazz music. When told he had incurable cancer, Michael sat down with her and asked for only two things; that his Sax be placed under his hands, in position in the casket, and that his favorite jazz cassettes be played during the visitation. The funeral director explained to his wife that this was not an unusual request. After Michael's death almost everyone who attended the visitation and funeral commented on how wonderful it was to see him with his beloved possession and hear his favorite music playing in the background. You could feel a sense of comfort that night and the next day at the service.

JOHN - At the service for a well-known member of a rock star group who was killed in an airplane crash, the survivors asked the funeral director to play only rock music since John was not religious and this type of music was important in his life.

RICHARD was an Irishman who grew up on the south side of Chicago and managed a pub for years. He was the outgoing type and wasn't afraid to let anyone know of his love for his Irish ancestry. He also liked to share drinks with friends. He asked one friend, a funeral director, to make sure that his funeral service was conducted like an old fashioned Irish wake. Richard died many years later after living what was said to be a long and joyful life. A private caterer showed up at the funeral home shortly before the wake and set up the bar and a food table. As family and friends arrived, there was a sense of loss but an even greater sense of celebration. Many toasts were made to Richard that night. Memories of friends and family were shared. Richard got the celebration of life he wanted.

DOROTHY was the matriarch grandmother and re-ferred to as Grandma Dorothy by her family. In her sweet manner she could get away with anything. The one thing that gave her strength was her dog, Tipper. He had been her constant companion since she was widowed years ago. She awoke one morning to find Tipper had died in his sleep and was overcome with grief. Her neighbors buried Tipper in the backyard where he had played.

Later she came up with an idea: have Tipper cremated and when she passed away, bury his cremains with her. She asked the funeral home if this was possible. The funeral director explained it was and came to her house, removed

Tipper from the yard and had him taken to the Pet Crematory for cremation. The funeral director and Dorothy agreed that Tipper's cremains would be placed in the casket in her hands, when she died, in a special container that Dorothy had made. Knowing they would be together again gave her great solace in dealing with the loss of her beloved companion, Tipper.

ROBERT was a very caring individual. At 62 he made pre-arrangements for his own funeral service and carefully detailed his wishes. He had never married and had lived and travelled all over the country in his sales job. His only family was a brother who lived in another state. After Robert died the funeral director checked his pre-arrangements and was surprised at his final wishes. Robert had requested cremation, with a memorial service for his brother and friends to follow. He wanted his cremains to be separated and scattered in nine different locations around the United States. The funeral home carried out these wishes, putting the cremains in nine separate containers and delivering them to the requested locations.

At the memorial service, Robert's brother and friends told of how he had touched their lives and his wonderful sense of humor. His brother asked the director how he knew so much about Robert's last wishes. The funeral director showed him Robert's file. His brother could not hold back the tears. He was overjoyed that Robert had taken such time and care ahead of time. He explained how his brother had been a perfectionist and always planned things in advance. "If Robert had not done this, I wouldn't have known what to do or what his final wishes were." Later, moved once again in life by his brother Robert, he made his own pre- arrangement plans.

Cremation

An example of new trends in cremation services is one that emerged this year in London. The Little Pub Company, indirectly inspired by the death of a customer at one of its pubs, initiated the idea. For $8,000 customers can have their ashes placed under their favorite stools or beneath the bar where they sat and be toasted every year as a not-quite-absent friend. Cremains can be accommodated anywhere in the pub. The fee includes an urn, a brass plaque, and the annual wake.

In Japan, where the majority of people are cremated, hi-tech rites are quickly replacing traditional funerals. In many funeral services, just prior to cremation, the motorized coffin, spotlighted by a laser and followed by the bereaved, glides toward a cascade of dry-ice fog to symbolize the deceased moving to another plane.

PLANNING A CEREMONY

In cases of unexpected death, where no pre-arrangements have been made, families are often at a loss as to what the wishes of the deceased might be. Some will rely on a minister to plan a service, others will request information from a funeral director. Increasingly, many wish to plan the service themselves. Following is an outline suggesting an approach to planning a funeral or memorial service for yourself, or for a loved one, whatever the circumstances.

Major Steps To Take

One - Decide who will take charge and do the planning. Will this be done by the minister or pastor, a family member, or a friend? Someone must lead the process.

Two - In private, before the service, the lead person should gather family and close friends together to discuss the life of the deceased. What did he love about life? What were his interests or hobbies? What were his goals, his hopes for the future? What was his contribution? What were his favorite hobbies, songs, music, literature, and poetry?

Encourage family and friends to talk about the happy times and events in the deceased's life that were cause for celebration. Ask for anecdotes about the person. Don't be afraid to bring out humor. What was the funniest thing this person ever said or did? This can trigger touching human stories about the deceased. A pattern will begin to emerge.

The loss of the loved one needs to be acknowledged, and most important, the survivors need to be left with a feeling of hope. By telling stories, both favorable and unfavorable, about the deceased in an intimate family setting, the survivors can begin the process of accepting the death.

Three - Determine what the mood of the ceremony is to be. Was this person religious? Would he prefer a traditional service? Would the deceased have wanted a celebration in his memory? Once this decision is reached, it will help in choosing readings and music. For example, a traditional Protestant funeral might include a reading of "The 23rd Psalm" or "The Lord's Prayer." A contemporary ceremony might use special music such as the service requested by the rock star. A humanist ceremony could include the deceased's philosophy of life.

Four - Decide where the ceremony will take place. Will it be in a church, a funeral home or other chapel? Perhaps it could be held outside in a park or other favorite location of the deceased.

Five - Decide who will deliver a eulogy or speak at the service. This could be a minister, a community leader or special friends and family of the deceased. Don't be afraid to ask if anyone would like to speak at the ceremony. Many people feel this is a way to honor a close friend.

Six - Decide on what the closing of the ceremony is to be. Will there be a graveside service? A scattering at sea? Often a minister will provide support to close family members immediately after the service. Some plan a special event, such as planting a tree over the buried cremains, or the scattering of cremains at sea. Is there to be a gathering of people to share a meal? If so, where will it be?

Memorial Service Pre-Planning Consideration
(For You OR Your Loved One)

1. Indicate your's or your loved one's goals, plans and dreams in life.

2. Whom do you want to invite to attend the service?

3. What are your major achievements?

4. What is your favorite music, poetry or literature?

5. What causes do you support? Do you want flowers at the ceremony? Do you want to release balloons at the end of the ceremony?

6. What do you love most in life? Nature? Animals? Drama? People?

7. Do you want a collage of your life with photos, slides, or a video?

8. Should personal letters be read?

9. Do you want to have food and drink served at a gathering after the service?

10. Should candles be lit to symbolize the light of life?

11. What people would you like to have speak?

12. Do you want a picture of yourself at the memorial service? A collage of pictures from infancy to death?

Whatever program is held, feel free to be creative. The service is for the survivors. Celebrate your loved one's life.

OUTLINE of a MEMORIAL or FUNERAL SERVICE

OPENING

Choose music and songs to set a mood. You may want to pick some of your loved one's favorites. They can be voice (soloist, choir, group) or instrumental (piano, harp, flute, organ, or guitar,) or recorded music.

READINGS

Readings from a religious service or certain scriptures may be read. You may also use requests from the deceased. The readings should acknowledge the loss of the loved one and offer support to the survivors.

MUSIC

Favorite music can be played during the service and highlighted at special times. The funeral participants could stand and sing hymns or songs together. A soloist might perform a particular selection asked for or liked by the deceased.

EULOGY

The designated speaker or speakers give a presentation. This should be personalized, remembering the deceased's life and accomplishments, offering hope and solace to the surviving family and friends. Those in attendance can offer their own testimonials to the deceased, remembering happy and sad times they shared together.

PRESENTATION Any other special presentations, such as photos, a video, or a slide show can be presented. Create what you need and want in order to memorialize your loved one and accept the passing. Use special music or read poems or sayings the deceased particularly liked or that portray his life. At some services, writings by the deceased are read. Family and friends may light candles from a single flame near the picture or coffin of the deceased.

CLOSING The lead person can say a few words or those in attendance may participate in singing as a group again.

GRAVESIDE Prayers can be said at the graveside for the deceased. Also, music can be used again after the clergyperson is finished. If a cremation occurred, a gathering for burial or the scattering of the cremains can take place.

CELEBRATION Family and friends gather together in the home, church, or a special place to share a meal in celebration of the loved one's life.

You may want to write out a Memorial Service for yourself or make notes on the outline listed on the following page and give a copy to your family or other loved ones. This will help you concretely think through your individual wishes and prepare your family, whether you are seriously ill or healthy. It will also allow you to be prepared in case of accidental or unexpected death.

OUTLINE FOR A MEMORIAL SERVICE

OPENING _____

_____

_____

_____

READINGS _____

_____

_____

_____

MUSIC _____

_____

_____

_____

EULOGY _____

_____

_____

_____

PRESENTATION _____

_____

_____

_____

CLOSING _____

_____

_____

_____

GRAVESIDE_____

_____

_____

CELEBRATION _____

_____

_____

CHAPTER 8

CONCLUSION

...A free man thinks of death least
of all things; and his wisdom is a
meditation not of death but of life...
— Spinoza

The Decision to Plan your Funeral

Most people wish for a peaceful and dignified end without pain and suffering. Each of us has the right to take control and plan the final ceremony of this last life process, to make the individual choices that will reflect our experiences in this life.

Making arrangements for your own funeral is an act of love, love for yourself by assuring that your final wishes are made known, and love for your family by easing the burden placed on them at an emotionally charged time. The decisions required in making funeral arrangements immediately after a loved one dies can leave family members upset and confused. Planning eliminates some major decisions and eases the pain.

In Closing

It is hoped that the information in this book will help you and your family to make the decisions required for a memorial or funeral ceremony, and to cope with the myriad demands surrounding the death of a loved one. It is designed to provide information to help you achieve dignified and affordable funeral arrangements. Its purpose is also to make known the need for bodies by medical schools for research and training and the procedures for organ donation. Following these guidelines—when they apply to your situation—will free you to devote yourself to grieving and to giving and receiving support from close relatives and friends. Knowing how to cope with the troublesome logistics, will bring peace of mind in the knowledge that you have carried out your loved one's wishes.

Whether you prefer burial, cremation, or bequeathal, have the courage to decide. Whether you want a traditional religious funeral service, a memorial service, or a committal service, be creative. There are no set rules. Discuss your plans with your family even though it may be difficult—for them and for you. Write your plans down. Sign and date your instructions and send copies to your next of kin or the person who will be responsible. If you belong to a memorial society, send a copy to them. Execute a will, a revocable trust if desired, a Living Will, or Durable Power of Attorney For Health Care. Take charge and control of the last act of your life, your final celebration.

For each of us death is the final act. No person can avoid it. Robert Kavanaugh, an ex-priest, teacher and psychologist said, "Never did I enjoy life more than when I finally began having the courage to face death." Look into your own heart for that courage. Peace!

RESOURCES

FOR DYING PATIENTS

Candlelighters (For Parents of
Children Dying of Cancer)
123 C. Street S.E.
Washington, DC 20003

I Can Cope
American Cancer Society
Director of Service and Rehabilitation
777 Third Ave.
New York, NY 10017

Make Today Count
PO Box 303
Burlington, IA 52601

National Hospice Organization
1901 Ft. Meyers Drive So.
Arlington, VA 22209

Share and Care
Cancer Education Coordinator
North Memorial Medical Center
3220 Lowry Avenue No.
Minneapolis, MN 55422

FOR AIDS PATIENTS
AIDS Project Los Angeles
3670 Wilshire Blvd. Suite 300
Los Angeles, CA 90010

Federation of Parents and Friends of
Lesbians and Gays (PFLAG)
Box 24565
Los Angeles, CA 90024

M.A.P. (Mothers of AIDS Patients)
P.O. Box 1763
Lomita, CA 90717

National Association of People With AIDS
1012 14th Street NW, Suite 601
Washington, DC

Nechama - A Jewish Response to AIDS
6000 W. Pico Blvd.
Los Angeles, CA 90035

The Los Angeles Shanti Foundation
6855 Santa Monica Blvd. Suite 408
Los Angeles, CA 90038

Shanti Project
890 Hayes St.
San Francisco, CA 94117

FOR CRIME VICTIMS

National Organization for Victim Assistance - NOVA
717 D. Street NW
Washington, DC 20004

National Victim Center
307 W. 7th St. Suite 1001
Fort Worth, TX 76102

Victims for Victims
1800 S. Robertson Blvd. Bldg. 6, Suite 400
Los Angeles, CA 90035

National Victim's Resource Center
PO Box 6000
Rockville, MD 20850

FOR THOSE WHO HAVE LOST AN INFANT OR CHILD

AAID
P.O. Box 20852
Milwaukee, WI 53220

A.M.E.N.D.
Aiding Mothers and Fathers Experiencing Neo-Natal Death
Maureen Connelly
4324 Berrywick Terrace
St. Louis, MO 63128

Centering Corporation
P.O. Box 3367
Omaha, NE 68103-0367
Information on those who have lost an infant or suffered miscarriage

Compassionate Friends
P.O. Box 3696
Oak Brook, IL 60522

Empty Arms
6416 Wyndham Ct.
Erie, PA 16505

Family Communications, Inc.
(Catalog of Mr. Rogers for children)
4802 Fifth Avenue
Pittsburg, PA 15213

MIDS, Inc.
16 Crescent Drive
Parsippany, NJ 07054

National Foundation for Sudden Infant Death
330 North Charles St.
Baltimore, MD 21201

National Sudden Infant Death Syndrome Foundation
P.O. Box 2474
Landover Hills, MD 20784

Parents of Murdered Children
100 East 8th St. Suite B41
Cincinnati, OH 45202

Parents of Prematures
Houston Organization for Parent Education
3311 Richmond Suite 330
Houston, TX 77098

Pregnancy & Infant Loss Center
1415 East Wayzata Blvd. Suite 22
Wayzata, MN 55391

S.H.A.R.E.
Source of Help in Airing and Resolving Experiences
St. John's Hospital
800 E. Carpenter
Springfield, IL 62769

FOR WIDOWED PERSONS

AARP Widowed Persons Service
1909 K Street NW
Washington DC 20049

Jewish Widows and Widowers
Beth El Temple Center
2 Concord Avenue
Belmont, MA 02178

NAIM Conference
2021 N. 60th St.
Milwaukee, WI 53208

Parents Without Partners
7910 Woodmont Avenue
Washington, DC 20014

Theos
They Help Each Other Spiritually
The Penn Hills Office Building
11609 Frankstown Rd. Room 306
Pittsburgh, PA 15235

SUICIDE

American Association of Suicidology
2459 South Ash
Denver, CO 80222

The Life Clinic
1026 S. Robertson Blvd.
Los Angeles, CA 90035

Ray of Hope
P.O. Box 2323
Iowa City, IA 52240

Survivors of Suicide
Sharry Schaefer
3251 N. 78th St.
Milwaukee, WI 53222

Suicide Prevention Center, Inc.
184 Salem Avenue
Dayton, OH 45406

Students Against Suicide
P.O. Box 115
South Laguna, CA 92677

Youth Suicide National Center
1825 I. Street NW Suite 400
Washington, DC 20006

GENERAL GRIEF

Accord Inc.
P.O. Box 5208
Louisville, KY 40205

Amend
4324 Berrywick Terrace
St. Louis, MO 63128

Grief Education
2422 So. Downing St.
Denver, CO 80210

Hand
P.O. Box 62
San Anselmo, CA 94960

Hoping
Sparrow Hospital
1215 E. Michigan Ave.
Lansing, MI 48909

Hoping and Sharing of Long Beach
5335 Carita Street
Long Beach, CA 90808

The Life Clinic
1026 S. Robertson Blvd.
Los Angeles, CA 90035

Prevention Center, Inc.
184 Salem Avenue
Dayton, OH 45406

Unite
Jeane's Hospital
7600 Central Avenue
Philadelphia, PA 19111

OTHER HELPFUL ORGANIZATIONS

American Cancer Society
777 Third Ave.
New York, New York 10017

Continental Assn. of Funeral & Memorial Societies
33 University Square, Suite 333
Madison, WI 53715
(800) 458-5563

Elizabeth Kubler Ross Center
So. Route 616
Head Waters, VA 2442

Foundation of Thanatology
630 W. 168th St.
New York, NY 10032

National Hemlock Society
P.O. Box 11830
Eugene, OR 97440-3900
(800) 247-7421

Loving Outreach for Survivors of Sudden Death
P.O. Box 7303
Stn. M. Edmonton, Alberta
Canada T5E 6C8

Make Today Count
For dying & terminally ill
P.O. Box 303
Burlington, IA 52601

Mended Hearts
721 Huntington Ave.
Boston, MA 02115
(For those who have had open
heart surgery)

Concern For Dying, Inc.
(For Example of Living Wills)
250 W. 57th St.
New York, NY 10107

Mothers Against Drunk Driving
MADD
511 E. John Carpenter Fwy., Suite 700
Irving, TX 75062
(214) 744-6233

Remove Intoxicated Drivers
RID
P.O. Box 520
Schenectady, NY 12301

National Hospice Organization
1901 North Fort Meyer Drive, Suite 402
Arlington, VA 22209

ORGAN DONATION AND BODY BEQUEATHAL

Below is a partial list of medical schools in the United States
and Canada. The list does not include all schools and more information can be obtained by contacting your own local medical schools, the American Medical Association or the
Canadian Medical Association.

UNITED STATES

Anatomical Gift Association of Illinois
2240 W. Fillmore St.
Chicago, IL 60612

University of Alabama
Anatomy Dept.
University Station
Birmingham, ALABAMA 35233

University of Arkansas
Anatomy Dept
Little Rock AR 72205

University of Arizona
College of Medicine
Anatomy Dept.
Tucson, AZ 86724

University of California at At Davis
School of Medicine
Davis, CA 95616

University of California at
Irvine - Anatomy Dept.
College of Medicine
Irvine, CA 92717

University of California at Los Angeles
School of Medicine
Dept. of Anatomy
Los Angeles, CA 90024

University of California at San Diego
School of Medicine
Learning Resources Office
La Jolla, CA 92093

Loma Linda - School of Medicine
Anatomy Dept.
Loma Linda, CA 92354

University of So. California
School of Medicine
1333 San Pablo St.
Los Angeles, CA 90033

Stanford University
School of Medicine
Stanford, CA 94305

University of California at San Francisco
Anatomy Dept.
San Francisco, CA 94143

University of Colorado
School of Medicine
4200 E. 9th Ave.
Denver, CO 80262

University of Connecticut
School of Medicine
Farmington Avenue
Farmington, CT 06032

Yale University
School of Medicine
New Haven, CT 06510

Georgetown University
Anatomy Dept.
Washington DC 20007

University of Hawaii
Dept. of Anatomy
1600 East-West Rd.
Honolulu, HI 96822

University of Iowa
Dept. of Anatomy
Iowa City, IA 52242

University of Kansas
Medical Center
39th & Rainbow Blvd.
Kansas City, KS 66103

University of Kentucky
College of Medicine
Lexington, KY 40292

Ohio State University
Anatomy Dept.
333 W. 10th Ave.
Columbus, OH 43210

Texas Tech University
Anatomy Dept.
Lubbock, TX 79430

Texas A & M University
Anatomy Dept.
College Station, TX 77843

Baylor College of Medicine
1200 Moursund
Houston, TX 77025

Duke Medical Center
Anatomy Dept.
Durham, NC 27710

University of Utah
School of Medicine
Salt Lake City, UT 84132

CANADA

University of Calgary
Faculty of Medicine
3350 Hospital Dr. NW
Calgary, ALTA T2N 4N1 Canada

University of Alberta
Faculty of Medicine
Edmonton, ALTA Canada

University of Ottawa
Anatomy Dept.
451 Smythe Rd.
Ottawa ONT K1H 8M5 Canada

University of Toronto
Anatomy Dept.
Faculty of Medicine
Toronto, ONT M5S 1A8 Canada

University of British Columbia
Faculty of Medicine
Vancouver, British Columbia Canada

Univ. de Montreal
Faculte de Med.
2900 Blvd. Edward Montpetit
Montreal, H3C 3J7 Canada

Univ. of Western Ontario
Dept of Anatomy
London ONT Canada

Univ. of Saskatchewan
College of Medicine, Anatomy Dept.
Saskatoon, SASK Canada

SPECIAL NEEDS

Brain Donations - There is a need for brain donations and other nerve tissues for research into Alzheimer's Disease. For information contact the National Alzheimer's Disease Brain Bank, c/o Dr. G. Glenner, University of California at San Diego, School of Medicine, La Jolla CA 92093.
In Canada, contact The Canadian Brain Tissue Bank, Room 128, Banting Institute, 100 College Street, Toronto, Ontario M5G 1L5.
Ear Drums - For information contact Project HEAR, 1801 Page Mill Road, Palo Alto, CA 94304 or the Ear Bank of British Columbia, 865 West 10th Ave., Vancouver, BC V5Z 1L7
Eye Glasses - New Eyes For The Needy, Box 332, 549 Millburn Ave. Short Hills, NJ 07078 accepts and distributes reusable eyeglasses through medical missions and hospitals overseas to the needy. Sales of donated frames, etc. fund new eyeglasses for U.S. recipients.
Eyes - There are eye banks all over the United States and in Canada. For a particular area consult your local telephone di-

rectory or information service. Some of the major organizations are:

UNITED STATES

Eyebank and Research Foundation, Inc.
1053 Buchanan St. NE
Washington DC 20017

Lions Doheny Eye Bank
1355 San Pablo St.
Los Angeles, CA 90033

New England Eye Bank
243 Charles St.
Boston, MA 02114

Sight Conversation Society of New York
628 Madison Avenue
Albany, NY 12208

Eye Bank For Sight Restoration
210 E. 64th St.
New York, NY 10021

CANADA

Eye Bank of Canada
B.C Division
CNIB
250 E. 36th Ave.
Vancouver BC V5W1C6 Canada

Eye Bank of Canada
Alberta Division
c/o CNIB
12010 Jasper Ave.
Edmonton, T5K 0P3   Canada

Eyebank of Canada
Ontario Division
1929 Bayview Ave.
Toronto M4G 3E8   Canada

La Banque D'Yeux Du Quebec
Maisoneuve-Rosemont Hospital
5689 Rosemont Blvd.
Montreal H1T 2H1   Canada

UNIFORM DONOR CARDS
You may obtain these forms from:

UNITED STATES

The Living Bank
PO Box 6725
Houston, TX 77265

Medic Alert
Turlock, CA 95380

Continental Association of
Funeral and Memorial Societies
33 University Square Suite #333
Madison, WI 53715

National Kidney Foundation
2 Park Avenue
New York, New York 10016

CANADA

Organ Donors Canada
5326 Ada Blvd.
Edmonton, Alberta T5W 4N7 Canada

Kidney Foundation of Canada
1650 de Maison neuve Blvd. W
Suite 400
Montreal, Quebec H3H 2PC Canada

FUNERAL AND MEMORIAL SOCIETIES

For a complete list of memorial societies in the United States contact the Continental Association of Funeral and Memorial Societies (CAFMS), 33 University Square, Suite 333, Madison, WI 53715.

This is a consulting society that provides information and publications on funerals and aging. They screen their members to make sure all are bona fide cooperative, democratic, non-profit, non discriminatory and committed to freedom of choice in funeral arrangements.

If there is no society near you can obtain information on forming one, if interested, by contacting CAFMS at the above address.

OTHER CONSUMER ORGANIZATIONS

Conference of Funeral Examining Boards
520 E. Van Trees St.
PO Box 497
Washington, IN 47501

This organization represents the licensing boards of 47 states and will provide information on the various laws and respond to consumer inquiries or complaints.

National Funeral Directors Association
11121 W. Oklahoma Avenue
Milwaukee, WI 53277
This is an organization of licensed funeral directors and funeral homes dedicated to the highest standards of funeral service. They can help with many facets of the funeral industry if you need to know about a funeral home in your area.

The American Cemetery Association
#3 Skyline Place Suite 1111
5201 Leesburg Pike
Falls Church, VA 22041
This is an organization of cemetery professionals that can help you with questions pertaining to cemetery matters or direct you to a cemetery in your area.

National Funeral Directors and Morticians Association
5723 South Indiana Avenue
Chicago, Illinois 60620
NFDMA is a national association primarily of black funeral providers.

National Selected Morticians
1616 Central Street
Evanston, Illinois 60201

NSM is a national association of funeral firms in which membership is by invitation only and is conditioned upon the commitment of each firm to comply with the association's Code of Good Funeral Practice.

Pre-Arrangement Interment Association of America
1133 15th Street N.W.
Washington, D.C. 20005
PIAA is a national association with more than 600 members in the cemetery and funeral home business whose purpose is to provide pre-arrangement purchases of funeral and cemetery goods and services.

ThanaCAP
135 West Wells Street, Suite 600
Milwaukee, Wisconsin 53203
ThanaCAP channels and arbitrates consumer complaints involving funeral directors.

Cremation Association of North America
111 East Wacker Drive
Chicago, Illinois 60601
CANA is an association of crematories, cemeteries, and funeral homes that offer cremation.

International Order of the Golden Rule
P.O. Box 3586
Springfield, Illinois 62708
OGR is an international association of independent funeral homes in which membership is by invitation only.

Jewish Funeral Directors of American, Inc.
122 East 42nd Street
New York, New York 10168
JFDA is a national trade association of funeral directors serving the Jewish community.

READING RESOURCES

American Association of Retired Persons, Consumer Affairs, Program Department - *Cemetery Goods And Services* and *Prepaying Your Funeral,* Some Questions To Ask, 1987, 1988.

Bradley, Buff, *Endings - A Book About Death,* Massachusetts, Addison-Wesley Publishing Co., 1979.

Channel Cities Memorial Society, *What You Should Know...What You Should Do...When Death Occurs,* Santa Barbara, CA., 1991.

Continental Association of Funeral and Memorial Societies, Inc. (CAFMS), and The Los Angeles Funeral Society, *A Multitude Of Voices - Funerals and The Clergy,* Los Angeles, 1980.

Cousins, Norman, *The Celebration of Life - A Dialogue on Immortality and Infinity.* New York, Harper & Row Publishers, 1974.

Department of Veteran Affairs, *Federal Benefits For Veterans And Dependents,* January 1991.

Federal Trade Commission/Bureau of Consumer Protection, *Consumer Guide To The FTC Funeral Rule,* Washington DC, 1984.

Humphrey, Derek, *Final Exit,* Hemlock Society, 1990.

Humphrey, Derek, *Let Me Die Before I Wake,* Los Angeles, The Hemlock Society, 1982.

Hyde, Margaret O. & Lawrence E., *Meeting Death.* New York, Walker and Company, 1989.

Kavanagh, Robert E., *Facing Death,* Los Angeles, Nash Publishing, 1972.

Lord, Janice Harris, *Beyond Sympathy*, Ventura, California, Pathfinder Publishing, 1990.

Lord, Janice Harris, *No Time For Goodbyes: Coping With Sorrow, Anger, And Injustice After A Tragic Death,* Ventura, California, Pathfinder Publishing, 1991.

Mitford, Jessica, *The American Way Of Death*, Simon and Shuster, New York, 1963.

Morgan, Ernest, *Dealing Creatively with Death, A Manual of Death Education and Simple Burial.* North Carolina, Celo Press, 1990.

National Funeral Directors Association, Inc., Milwaukee, WI. NFDA Learning Resources Center: Pamphlets available on funerals and related subjects.

Parrish-Hara, Rev. Carol W., *The New Age Handbook on Death And Dying,* Santa Monica, California, IBS Press, 1989.

Raab, Dr. Robert A., *Coping With Death,* New York, The Rosen Publishing Group, Inc., 1989.

Rich, Christine and Deanna Kessler, *Walking With You,* Liberty Mo., R.C.R. Publications, 1988.

Zim, Herbert S. and Sonia Bleeker, *Life And Death,* New York, William Morrow and Son, 1970.

GRIEF READING RESOURCES

Carlson, Lisa. *Caring for Your Own Dead*, Upper Access Publishers, One Upper Access Road, P. O. Box 457, Hinesburg, VT. 05461.

Donnelly, Katherine F. *Recovering From the Loss of a Child,* Macmillan Publishing Co., 866 3rd Ave., New York, NY 10022.

Grollman, Earl A. *Living When a Loved One has Died,* Beacon Press/Fitzhenry & Whiteside Ltd., Toronto, Canada.

Grollman, Earl A. *What Helped Me When My Loved One Died.* Beacon Press, 25 Beacon Street, Boston, Massachusetts 02108.

Grollman, Earl A. *Talking About Death: A Dialogue Between Parent and Child,* Beacon Press, 25 Beacon Street, Boston, Massachusetts, 02108.

Hewett, John. *After Suicide*, Westminster Press, Philadelphia, PA.

Kubler-Ross, Elisabeth. *On Children and Death,* Macmillan Publishing Company, 866 Third Avenue, New York, NY 10022.

Manning, Doug. *What to Do When You Lose a Loved One,* Harper & Row, 151 Union St., San Francisco, CA 94111-1299.

Osterweis, Marian et al Eds. *Bereavement: Reactions, Consequences and Care,* National Academy Press, 2101 Constitution Avenue NW, Washington, D.C. 20418.

Rando, Therese A. *Parental Loss of a Child,* Research Press, 2612 N. Mattis, Champaign, IL 61821.

Rando, Therese A. *Grieving: How to Go on Living When Someone You Love Dies,* Lexington Books, 125 Spring St., Lexington, MA 02173.

Ross, Betsy E. *After Suicide: A Unique Grief Process*, Betsy Ross, Iowa City, Iowa.

Schiff, Harriet S. *The Bereaved Parent,* Penguin Books, 40 W. 23rd Street, New York, NY 10010.

Schiff, Harriett S. *Living Through Mourning,* Viking-Penguin, 40 W. 23rd St., New York, NY 10010.

Westberg, Granger E. *Good Grief*, Fortress Press, Philadelphia, PA.

Staudacher, Carol. *Beyond Grief: A Guide for Recovering from the Death of a Loved One,* New Harbinger Publications, 2200 Adeline St., Suite 305, Oakland, CA 94607.

When Hello Means Goodbye (when infants die before, during or shortly after birth) Perinatal Loss, 2116 NE 18th Avenue, Portland, OR 97212.

INDEX

DETACHABLE FORMS FOR YOUR PERSONAL PAPERS

INSTRUCTIONS TO FOLLOW UPON MY DEATH

Pre-arrangement Information

I have prepared the following information to assist my loved ones in handling my final arrangements. Please follow through with what I have written. Do not change any of my last wishes unless the changes cannot be avoided. Thank you.

Personal Information

Name_____ Date_____

Address _____

_____

City_____State _____

Social Security Number: _____

Date of Birth: _____

Place of Birth:_____

Date of Marriage: _____

Place of Marriage: _____

Father's Name and birthplace (addresses and telephone numbers if living): _____

_____

Mother's Name and birthplace (addresses and telephone numbers if living):_____

_____

Major places and number of years of residence:

Locally: _____

Other: _____

_____

Education, list and dates of degrees received:

High School: _____

College:_____

Post Graduate: _____

Other: _____

Work Experience: _____

_____

_____

Employer: _____

Job Title:_____

From (Date):_____To (Date): _____

Date of Retirement: _____

Veteran Information:

Branch of Service: _____

Wars Served: _____

Medals or Special Service:_____

_____

Place and Date Entered Service: _____

Date of Discharge: _____

Rank and Serial Number: _____

Organization or outfit:_____

Location of discharge papers: _____

Flag desired to drape casket: Yes: No:

Religious Affiliation:

Religion: _____

Church Affiliation: _____

Professional or Fraternal organization:.

Other Organizations/Special Interests: _____

_____

_____

Additional information/remarks: _____

_____

_____

_____

_____

Funeral Arrangements

Name_____

Autopsy Permission

I will permit autopsy (unless authorities require it).

____Yes ____No

Relatives and Friends to Notify

(Names, addresses, and telephone numbers)

Survivors:

Spouse: _____

_____

_____

Parents: _____

Children: _____

_____

_____

_____

Brothers: _____

_____

_____

Sisters: _____

_____

_____

Names, addresses and telephone numbers of friends to notify:

_____

_____

Number of Nieces: ____Number of Nephews:____

Number of Grandchildren: ____

Number of Great-Grandchildren:____

Donations to be made in my memory: _____

_____

_____

_____

_____

Pallbearers I Would Like: _____

_____

_____

_____

_____

Honorary Pallbearers: _____

_____

_____

_____

Others to notify of my death: _____

_____

_____

_____

_____

_____

Any additional instructions or considerations not included in the list above: _____

_____

_____

_____

_____

_____

_____

_____

Signed By:

_____

Date:_____

Witnessed By:

_____

Location of Important Information, Papers, and Documents

Name_____

Location of will: _____

_____

_____

The name , address, and telephone number of legal advisor: _

_____

_____

Location of safety deposit box and key: _____

_____

_____

Bank trust department: _____

_____

Location of all checking and savings accounts (address and branch No., Acct. No.): _____

_____

_____

_____

_____

_____

_____

_____

Location of checkbooks and passbooks: _____

_____

_____

_____

_____

_____

Credit cards and charge accounts to be cancelled: _____

_____

_____

_____

_____

Insurance policies and Location: _____

_____

_____

_____

Location of Service Discharge Papers:_____

_____

Trusts in effect:_____

_____

_____

_____

Funeral pre-arrangements if made (Power of Attorney): __

_____

_____

My Executor/Executrix is: _____

_____

My Physician is: _____

_____

_____

Living Will: _____

Durable Power of Attorney for Health Care: _____

_____

Additional items: _____

_____

_____

_____

_____

_____

_____

_____

PRE-ARRANGED FUNERAL SERVICE INFORMATION

Name_____ Date_____

My Service is to be held at: _____

Clergy: _____

Church, Funeral Home, or special place: _____

Special Music: _____
_____

Organist/Soloist/Other: _____
_____

I would like the eulogy said by: _____
_____

I wish to be cremated. (See separate Cremation form)_____

Visitation location and time: _____

Casket should be open: _____closed: _____

Casket I prefer: _____
_____

Outer enclosure (vault) I prefer: _____
_____

Cemetery to be used and instructions: _____
_____

Cemetery lot: Section: _____

Lot:_____Block:_____Space: _____

Committal at grave side: _____

Clothing to use: _____
_____

Jewelry I wish to wear: _____
_____

Instructions for disposition of jewelry before burial: _____

Flowers or Memorial Donation: _____
_____

Other special instructions: _____
_____

CREMATION INFORMATION SHEET

Name: _____

I Wish To be Cremated: _____Yes_____No

I wish there to be a visitation and/or service before I am cremated: _____Yes_____No

I would like to have a memorial service after cremation:

_____Yes_____No

If yes, where: _____

I would like to have my cremains returned in an urn: _____

Type of Urn: _____Price Range: _____

I would like my cremains buried:_____Yes_____No

If yes, where: _____

I would like my cremains scattered:_____Yes_____No

If yes, where:_____

(Please check with your funeral director for legal requirements.)

I do/do not have a pacemaker: _____

I wish my cremains returned to: Name: _____

_____

I prefer direct cremation with no service: _____

I prefer direct cremation with a memorial service following: _

_____

I do/do not want my cremains at the memorial service: _____

I would like to have a picture of me placed in view at my memorial service: _____

It is located at: _____

Description of Picture:_____

_____

_____

Flowers or Memorial Donation: _____

Please remove all jewelry before cremation and return to: __

_____

132

ORGAN DONATION FORM

Name: _____

After Death I Prefer To Donate These organs:

_____

_____

TO (organization): _____

_____

_____

Autopsy (If family or doctor requests): _____

That my body be donated to:_____

_____

Date of Arrangements: _____

_____

Location of paperwork:_____

_____

Contact:_____

_____

_____

Name_____

Signed_____

Date_____

NOTES

ORDER FORM

Pathfinder Publishing of California
458 Dorothy Ave.
Ventura, CA 93003
Telephone (805) 642-9278   FAX (805) 650-3656

Please send me the following books from Pathfinder Publishing:

____Copies of **Agony & Death on a Gold Rush Steamer** @ $8.95	$____
____Copies of **Beyond Sympathy** @ $9.95	$____
____Copies of **Dialogues In Swing** @ $12.95	$____
____Copies of **Final Celebrations** @ $9.95	$____
____Copies of **Let Your Ideas Speak Out** @ $8.95	$____
____Copies of **Life With Charlie** @ $9.95	$____
____Copies of **Living Creatively With Chronic Illness** @ $11.95	$____
____Copies of **More Dialogues In Swing**	
Softcover @ $14.95	$____
Hardcover @ $22.95	$____
____Copies of **No Time For Goodbyes** @ $9.95	$____
____Copies of **Quest For Respect** @ $7.95	$____
____Copies of **Stop Justice Abuse** @ $10.95	$____
____Copies of **Surviving a Japanese POW Camp** @ $11.95	$____
____Copies of **Shipwrecks, Smugglers & Maritime Mysteries** @ $9.95	$____
____Copies of **World of Gene Krupa** @ $14.95	$____
Sub-Total	$____
Californians: Please add 7.25% tax.	$____
Shipping*	$____
Grand Total	$____

I understand that I may return the book for a full refund if not satisfied.

Name:_____

Address:_____

_____ZIP:_____

*SHIPPING CHARGES U.S.
Books: Enclose $2.50 for the first book and .50c for each additional book. UPS: Truck; $3.50 for first item, .50c for each additional. UPS Air: $5.00 for first item, $1.50 for each additional item.